Secular Hope

What the Religious Right really wants and Why Liberal Democrats Should Support Them

Andrea L. Parliament

iUniverse, Inc.
New York   Bloomington

Secular Hope
What the Religious Right really wants and Why
Liberal Democrats Should Support Them

iUniverse books may be ordered through booksellers or by contacting:

iUniverse
1663 Liberty Drive
Bloomington, IN 47403
www.iuniverse.com
1-800-Authors (1-800-288-4677)

Because of the dynamic nature of the Internet, any Web addresses or links contained in this book may have changed since publication and may no longer be valid.

ISBN: 978-1-4401-9391-0 (sc)
ISBN: 978-1-4401-9392-7 (ebk)

Library of Congress Control Number: 2009912505

Printed in the United States of America

iUniverse rev. date: 4/7/2010

Dedicated to Marjorie Mercy and William Daniel

Beauty is Truth, truth beauty

That is all

Ye know on Earth,

And all ye need to know.

John Keats
– Ode to A Grecian Urn –

Acknowledgements

First, I would like to thank Harvey Cox for his books which so gracefully blend academic excellence with compassion. His works have both allowed me, and inspired me, to see beyond the wall of separation. Second, I gratefully acknowledge the late Dr. Michael Enzle, my honours supervisor at the University of Alberta, who taught me how to conduct excellent research.

Next I would like to thank my former colleagues at the Alberta Women's Secretariat, Ontario's Ministry of Finance, and the Canadian Banker's Association for the opportunity to learn and finesse the art of public policy formation.

I am grateful to Brendan Bailey for our fast-paced and inspiring conversations and for introducing me to the work of Jürgen Habermas. I also would like to thank Yury Lyubchenko for his technical support and expertise.

To Denise Alberts and her sister Francine, my heartfelt appreciation for a beautiful piece of art that has been silently encouraging me for years. I am grateful for Alexis Reiter, my favorite calligrapher, who wisely sent me off to law school with the advice "Know Thyself". I would also like to thank Marion Hinteregger for her excellent marketing advice, unfailing optimism and beautiful friendship.

I am deeply grateful to my father for sharing his love of old books, providing his example of being his own person and for being a learned sounding board as I struggled to formulate my ideas. My mother's loving support, perseverance and dedicated public service will *always* serve as a never-ending source of inspiration to me.

Finally, I wish to express my deep appreciation to Karl for his keen eye in finding the right books, his insightful social commentary that opened up my mind and heart to hearing another perspective, and most importantly for convincing me to overcome my Canadian reticence and appreciate the importance of fighting for truth.

CONTENTS

INTRODUCTION

It was not until this book was nearly complete that I realized one of the motivations for writing *Secular Hope* stemmed from a remark made by a law professor of mine in 1995. Responding to questions from his first-year class as to where the system went wrong in the OJ Simpson trial, the professor replied "Welcome to the school of law, not the school of justice". His comment revealed my profession's systemic lack of commitment to objective truth, and hence its failure to deliver justice. I now understand this attitude to be a significant cause of the global religious resurgence.

My view of the religious right, which I define as those who seek a basic level of agreement between their religious and legal moral codes, has recently changed for the better. My first troubling experience was in the mid-1990s while I was working at the YWCA, running a program for abused women. I had learned of some religious groups requesting equal government funding for their organizations. Given the life and death nature of the services that shelters provided, I did not understand why the comparison was being drawn and so dismissed them as anti-feminist, religious extremists.

My second negative experience concerned the tax credit for private schools introduced by Jim Flaherty in Ontario in 2001. As a good Canadian, I was horrified at the prospect of our children's education being separated along religious lines. It was then that I started to research how the Canadian Constitution protected its secular nature. I became distressed when I failed to find the Canadian version of the American anti-establishment clause and a few months later the twin towers fell. And a few years after that, George W. Bush was elected to a second term. By this time, I was now concerned about *my* growing intolerance and cynicism as I heard myself say things like "Bush must have rigged Florida, because even half of America could not possibly be that stupid".

Then one day, when I was trying to decide whether Canada should join America in the war against terrorism, I was struck by my own reaction which was to lean on my religious teaching of "turn the other cheek", as opposed to my legal training which told me that liberal democracies had no defense against the intolerant; therefore we should retaliate with significant pre-emptive force. The sin of pride held me back. Did we really do everything we could to prevent this war? What if the problem was our inability to understand how we were inadvertently hurting others? I started to think more deeply about the relationship between religion and reason.

My moment of clarity came when I was humble enough to admit that my reasoning could fail and that religion was most helpful in determining when reasoning was failing. *Faith* took on a deeper meaning. As neither praying nor bombing Iraq seemed quite right or adequate, I started to read everything I could about secularization and I put my faith in the humanity of my enemies and in our collective ability to reason.

Because a favorite family pastime was to frequent used bookstores, it was my good fortune to start with Harvey Cox's 1965 best-seller *The Secular City*, wherein he warned America not to confuse secularism with secularization. It was not an easy distinction to grasp, so it haunted me. I looked unsuccessfully for many years for any follow-up commentary in the academic literature. It was in reviewing the legal jurisprudence that I realized that inconsistent definitions of secular were the source of much conflict.

In trying to understand my own country's version of secularity, it was impossible not to be drawn to the work that was written for America. Often, it is when trying to understand others that we can most accurately see ourselves. I learned that the greatest difference between our two countries is that the United States was founded on faith in secularization, while Canada amended its Constitution in 1982, thereby recasting its future on faith in Postmodern Secularism.

Secularization is the long-term faith in one objective moral truth uniting all human beings. Postmodern Secularism is the long-term faith in tolerance. Secularization requires faith in religion, our ability to reason and a long term-perspective. Secularism requires cynicism, faith in the judiciary and a fear of absolutes. That said, secularization is deeply embedded in all monotheistic cultures; it cannot be easily abandoned even with the best of intentions.

I no longer see the religious resurgence as a sign of secularization's failure, but of its success. The religious resurgence is a sign of *secularism's* failure. Secularization is the transferring of moral authority to individuals and I believe that liberal democracies should attempt to make philosopher kings of all its citizens. Secularization will bring all citizens to a much deeper understanding of our own human nature, so that collectively we can achieve a higher level of consciousness and become morally accountable, as will be required to deal with the enormous global dilemmas of bioethics and global warming.

My deepest wish is that the new metaphors and terminology in *Secular Hope* inspire America to refine, and reclaim, its unique secular history. I believe that through a strong commitment to secularization America can, and will, peacefully lead the world into the post-secular era.

This research journey seriously challenged my own identity as a tolerant, liberal Canadian. In reading the finer details of

American constitutional history and case law, there were many moments when I had to reluctantly admit the merit of arguments that I had previously cynically dismissed. While I have become a big fan of the American Constitution, I am still claiming a Canadian identity as I have emerged with tolerance for "the intolerant" and I hope to have played a role more consistent with Canada's peacekeeping reputation. Finally, I am happy to report that while I still watch and enjoy the Daily Show, my cynicism is gone. This is how my faith lets me know when I have stopped subjectively rationalizing and started to objectively reason. My mind and soul are at peace, and my vision of the future is bright.

Chapter 1 – America and Its Discontents

America Increasingly Divided

Metaphors are words with power. Americans built a metaphoric wall to separate religion from politics, only to find that in the 2000 Presidential election, religion was the strongest predictor of who voted for George W. Bush. During the 2008 presidential campaign, the pastor at Barack Obama's church received more media attention than the enormous credit problem that imploded, spawning a global recession. And as of November, 2009, Americans' religious intensity continued to be a major predictor of party identification and approval of President Obama's performance.[1] Are the ancient Roman gods who ruled for over 1,100 years laughing at young America's secular attempt to control its own fate?

The constitutional wall was designed to separate institutions, but now it is separating U.S. citizens. In 2009, America divided fairly evenly into left and right: with 47 percent of Americans identifying themselves as progressive/liberal and 48 percent as conservative/Libertarian.[2] This split is increasingly becoming geographical, with the West coast and Northeast being predominantly progressive/liberal and the Southern interior and Southeastern states being conservative/Libertarian. Further, Americans are no longer moving once they become settled: only 12 percent of Americans changed residences in 2007, the smallest number since tracking commenced in the late 1940's.[3]

While America's Second Civil War was declared by Ronald Brownstein in 2007,[4] it really started thirty-four years earlier, in 1973. That year the IRS attempted to rescind the tax-exempt status of Bob Jones University for its racial discrimination policies. In response, Paul Weyrich founded the Heritage Foundation for the promotion of libertarian policies on taxation and regulation. By 1979, Weyrich broke the spirit of the wall of separation by partnering with Jerry Falwell, who also broke with his Baptist Church's long standing tradition of separating church and state.

This movement gained momentum as a consequence of the Supreme Court decisions to remove school prayers, legalize abortion and overturn sodomy laws. Soon the infamous Moral Majority was founded such that when the constitutional wall reached its apex in the 1980's, the religous right was able to scale it back by electing Ronald Reagan.

The political marriage between Libertarians and the religious right has lasted over thirty years, the fruits of which are many religiously inspired policy changes. In 1996 Congress provided special funding for abstinence-only sex education programs and the Defense of Marriage Act (DOMA) was passed to restrict the definition of marriage to the union of a man and a woman; in 2002 the Supreme Court deemed indirect religious school funding through voucher programs constitutional; President Bush vetoed stem cell research funding in 2006; in 2007 the Supreme Court upheld Bush's Partial Birth Abortion Act, ruling that laws limiting abortions need not include an exemption clause protecting the health of the mother; and finally, in 2008, President Bush passed a Conscience Clause for medical workers allowing them to abstain from conducting public services for religious reasons.

While President Obama's election brought the art of compromise back to the White House, the Second Civil War continues on different fronts. Obama is reaching out to the religious right by demonstrating his fluency in the language of religious scripture, while trying to avoid religious rationale for his policy positions. In his inaugural address he stated "We remain a young nation, but in the words of the Scripture, the time has come to set aside childish things". As a second example, he referenced Christ's "Sermon on the Mount" in a speech warning America not to rebuild its economic future on a pile of sand. In a more troubling example however, during his acceptance speech for the Nobel Peace Prize, Obama used the religious term "evil" to justify war, although he tempered his comments with subsequent commitments to international law and standards in regard to the use of force and torture.

President Obama has demonstrated his commitment to secular values by ending funding for the abstinence-only sex-education programs, reversing the stem cell funding policy, and committing to extending full material benefits to same-sex civil unions at the federal level. However, in a seemingly contradictory move he filed legal briefs in support of the DOMA in June, 2009, and has taken no action in removing the "Don't Ask, Don't Tell" military policy as of December, 2009. Obama has also reconsidered his promise to reverse a policy allowing religious organizations that receive federal funds, to discriminate in their hiring practices on the basis of religion.

Are Obama's policies just carefully crafted rhetoric designed to appease both sides of America's divide? Consider, for example, Obama's compromise on same-sex marriage: equal material rights at the federal level, while protecting a heterosexual definition of marriage. The result is that the issue moves to the state level – reinforcing the wall of separation dividing America. Tony Perkins, president of the Family Research Council, a conservative Christian organization, told the *New York Times* that the California ballot initiative on same-sex marriage was more important than the presidential election. And while the Supreme Court of Iowa overturned a ten-year-old statutory ban on same-sex marriages in April, 2009, it is expected that the issue will be the wild card in the 2010 Iowa elections. The metaphoric wall continues to deeply divide the country into "red" and "blue" states.

ACADEMIC CHANGE OF HEART

America's constitutional discontents are no longer limited to the religious right. Even atheists are giving up on the wall of separation as an effective constitutional doctrine. Sam Harris lamented, in his 2004 best-selling book, *End of Faith,* "It is time that we recognized that belief is not a private matter; it has never been merely private."[5] Harris is indirectly stating that the separation of church and state is not *really* possible because the line between public and private gets blurred on Election Day. So Harris predicted:

> We will see that the greatest problem confronting civilization is not merely religious extremism: rather it is the larger set of cultural and intellectual accommodations we have to faith itself. Religious moderates are, in large part, responsible for the religious conflict in our world, because their beliefs provide the context in which scriptural literalism and religious violence can never be adequately opposed.[6]

In making this comment, Harris is arguing that the separation of church and state should apply not only to institutions or government employees, but also to private citizens. This is no small request considering it would be contrary to the freedom of conscience and religion that prompted the American constitutional experiment in the first place. However, Harris' comments echo those of the influential liberal philosopher John Rawls, who suggested that citizens should not vote, based on their religious beliefs, because rational explanations are owed to other citizens when their freedoms are curtailed in a secular society. While most defenders of liberalism, including Alan Wolfe, want to distance themselves from Harris' strong rhetoric and Rawls' cold logic which can approach educational elitism, they are forced to acknowledge the political risks of tolerating citizens who are not themselves tolerant. The American constitution is under considerable pressure to balance the increasingly divergent demands of the political left and right.

Raising the constitutional stakes from yet another perspective is Wendy Brown, a political scientist from Berkeley. In her 2006 book, *Regulating Aversion*, Brown challenged the idea that the secular value of tolerance is universally neutral. Brown claims tolerance is a Western value that is ultimately used to justify discrimination and violence against people from other cultures. This is a significant challenge to the West because secular tolerance is the only political principle that can simultaneously respect, and yet contain, religious beliefs.

Another American academic, anthropologist Talal Asad of the City University of New York, makes the same argument in a less contentious manner. He suggests that secularism, which requires a separation of private beliefs from public discourse, essentially excludes Islamic citizens from meaningful political participation. Asad recommends that for Muslims to be adequately represented in secular societies, their cultural memories and traditions must be integrated into political institutions. What this would mean in the way of necessary compromises is not clear. In a similar line of reasoning, philosopher Charles Taylor, in his report on religious accommodation in the Canadian province of Quebec, makes his argument for "open secularism" such that those with religious beliefs can play a larger role in public life.

Even the secularization scholars have abandoned the secularists in their attempt to shore up the wall of separation. Secularization theory was academically popular until the late 1980's. It predicted that religious values would diminish as globalization, urbanization and technology challenged the universality of one's religious claims and science continued to disprove myth. This trend was considered irreversible and the hallmark of modernity since the Enlightenment.

However, in the face of significant evidence of a global resurgence consisting of a Christian Protestant movement in the United States, South America and Africa, as well as a resurgence of Islam around the world, most of the secularization scholars changed their minds. Peter Berger, a sociologist at Boston University, reversed his opinion on the irreversible trend in the late 1980's[7] and Harvey Cox, the Harvard theologian best known for his book *The Secular City,* has more recently pronounced that "secularization is dead".[8] And in 1994, sociologist Jose Casanova, from Georgetown University, asked "Who still believes in the myth of secularization?"[9]

SECULARISM LITE

But not all academics have given up secular hope. Some are hoping this is a temporary blip, not a sustained return to religious beliefs. Work is being done to deconstruct the nuances of the terms secularism, religion, and modernity in order to revive the irreversible march toward progress. Pollsters have set up networks in every corner of the world to monitor changes in religious attitudes, behaviors, and policies in order to explain the secularization theory with increasingly detailed nuances. Secularization is usually measured as the frequency of church attendance and prayer, self-identified religious affiliation if any, and belief in God. The data convincingly shows an economic foundation to secularization because there is a clear international trend of stronger economies having higher rates of atheism, and poorer countries having stronger intensity of religious beliefs.[10]

This correlation is very strong in Europe, where religious beliefs are at an all-time low and economic development is relatively high. Religion is also most intensely practiced in the world's poorest nations, such as Senegal, Ethiopia, Nigeria, and Indonesia. However, there is a clear outlier to this global trend—the United States. In 2006, while the United States had GDP per capita at $50,000, it had levels of religious intensity similar to Poland and Mexico whose GDP per capita were one-fifth of the United States. Given that the United States was the first to adopt a secular constitution, it is unclear if America is just an outlier or a predictor of what is to come.

In recanting the secularization theory, Peter Berger explained the overall global resurgence as having three sources: (1) the human need for certainty, (2) secularism as the view of a powerful educated elite, and (3) "strongly felt religion has always been around."[11] However, the problem with Berger's three explanations is that none of them can explain why there was a decline in the United States up until the 1970s and why the United States would differ from other Western countries.

In trying to explain the U.S. exception, a joint study from Harvard and University of Michigan concluded that the United States' religious revival likely stems from America's poor social welfare system:

> The US is exceptionally high in religiosity in large part, we believe, because it is also one of the most unequal post-industrial societies under comparison. Exceptionally high levels of economic insecurity are experienced by many sectors of US society, despite American affluence, due to the cultural emphasis on the values of personal responsibility, individual achievement, and mistrust of big government, limiting the role of public services and the welfare state for

7

basic matters such as healthcare covering all the
working population. [12]

The problem with the economic development, or secularism
lite theory, is that unlike the underlying forces of the secularization
theory (globalization, urbanization and technology); economic
development does not have an irreversible linear progression.

Are we regressing to the religious wars that plagued Europe
in the sixteenth and seventeenth centuries because of a returning
income gap between rich and poor? Such an explanation would
be nice and simple, but in America it is the religious right that is
preventing the regulatory reform that would rectify this problem.
If religious views are held most intensely by the less educated and
the poor, why would they be resisting the social reforms offered
by liberal Democrats? The cause of the religious resurgence is not
yet understood.

THE CLASH OF RELIGIOUS CIVILIZATIONS?

In addition to the domestic attacks on the Constitutional Wall,
American secularism is considered by some Muslims to be a direct
threat to Islam. America's foreign policy of spreading democracy,
freedom, and secular values has not been welcomed, but rather
interpreted as threats to Islamic values. Samuel P. Huntington,
in his 1996 best-selling book *The Clash of Civilizations and the
Remaking of the World Order*, predicted Western and Islamic
cultures to be the most prone to cultural clashes. The September
11, 2001, attacks on the World Trade Center and the Pentagon,
America's symbols of Western progress and globalization, gave
Huntington's thesis credibility. Huntington argued that the sources
of this conflict are the uniquely Western events of the Christian
Reformation, the Renaissance, and the Enlightenment.

Most scholars support the Reformation as the critical historical
event that split Islam with the West, because the Reformation

took power away from both church and state and placed it with the individual. Northrop Frye, a biblical scholar, pointed to the Reformation as the distinguishing Western event that established the legitimacy of an individual's democratic right to participate politically:

> Just as the Protestant church subordinates itself to the impact of Scripture, so in temporal matters it subordinates itself to the "higher powers," without claiming temporal authority. This renunciation extrudes the society of power from the Church itself, which thereupon builds itself up on the pattern of Christian liberty, forming an apostolic community in which members are made free and equal by their faith.[13]

Similarly, John Rawls identified the Reformation as the critical historical event that spawned the works of Locke and Mill, and hence Western liberal democracies. In *A Secular Age*, philosopher Charles Taylor outlined the Western cultural changes since the 1500's that allowed for a complete reversal of the social conditions that now make it almost impossible *to believe* in God. Bernard Lewis stated, "Generally speaking, Muslim tolerance of unbelievers was far better than anything available in Christendom, until the rise of secularism in the seventeenth century."[14] Reformation-based explanations for the culture clash are also supported by a general pattern of lagging secularization in traditionally Catholic countries like Poland, Ireland and many countries in South America. Further, the leading secularist countries in northern Europe, like Sweden, for example, have traditionally Protestant backgrounds.

However, these reformation-based explanations fail to consider that Islam is not a hierarchical religion, but has always advocated that individuals have direct relationships with their god Allah. Further, the reformation-based explanation cannot explain why America's religious resurgence is almost exclusively Protestant.[15]

Finally, it needs to be explained how the many traditionally Catholic countries like Ireland and Spain so quickly reverted to extreme secularism without similarly reforming events.

According to Berger the Secularism Lite theory does not explain the Islamic resurgence either:

> An important characteristic of the Islamic revival is that it is by no means restricted to the less modernized or "backward" sectors of society, as progressive intellectuals still like to think. On the contrary, it is very strong in cities with a high degree of modernization, and in a number of countries it is particularly visible among people with Western-style higher education; in Egypt and Turkey, for example, it is often the daughters of secularized professionals who are putting on the veil and other accoutrements expressing so-called Islamic modesty.[16]

Our failure to understand secularization has caused, and continues to cause, serious problems for both America's domestic and foreign policies. The role of secularization in the development of civilization is far from universally agreed upon. Sadly, many moderate Muslims become cynical when confronted with America's inability to explain their own secular inconsistencies, as Thomas Friedman reported in his *New York Times* article of October 2005:

> A delegation of Iraqi judges and journalists abruptly left the United States today, cutting short its visit to study the workings of American democracy.
>
> A delegation spokesman said the Iraqis were "bewildered" by some of the behavior of the Bush administration and felt it was best to limit

their exposure to the U.S. system at this time, when Iraq is taking its first baby steps towards democracy.

The lead Iraqi delegate, Muhammed Mithaqi, a noted secular Sunni judge who recently survived an assassination attempt by Islamist radicals, said he was stunned when he heard President George W. Bush telling Republicans that one reason they should support Harriet Miers for the U.S. Supreme Court was because of "her religion."

Mithaqi said that, after two years of being lectured to by U.S. diplomats about the need to separate "mosque from state" in the new Iraq, he was so floored to read that former Whitewater prosecutor Kenneth Starr, now a law school dean, said on conservative James Dobson's radio show that Miers deserved support because she was "a very, very strong Christian (who) should be a source of great comfort and assistance to people in the households of faith around the country".

"Now, let me get this straight," Mithaqi said. "You are lecturing us about keeping religion out of politics, and then your own president and conservative legal scholars go and tell your public to endorse Miers as a Supreme Court justice because she is an evangelical Christian?

"Is that the Iraq you sent your sons to build and die for?" [17]

Such international incidents only make America's domestic divide even greater. With contradictions such as these, it is not difficult to see how even moderate Muslims would view American foreign policy as thinly veiled monotheistic imperialism. While the anti-secular bias of President Bush was clear, President Obama is continuing with many of Bush's faith-based initiatives domestically, while fighting the Taliban abroad.

Is religious accommodation a slippery slope to be avoided at all costs and therefore the wall of separation should be even higher? Or is the secular wall of separation an outdated ideology which, like the Iron Curtain, is destined to fall? America's political problems reflect profoundly different ideas about what the path of progress looks like and unfortunately until a universal concept of progress is agreed upon, there shall be limited peace for America, both domestically and internationally.

NOTES

1. A new Gallup analysis of more than 29,000 interviews Gallup conducted in November found that Republicans outnumbered Democrats by 12 percentage points among Americans who are classified as highly religious, while Democrats outnumber Republicans by 30 points among those who are not religious. Highly religious white Americans were more than twice as likely as those who are not religious to disapprove of Obama's job performance. December 11, 2009, "Religious Intensity Remains Powerful Predictor of Politics" by Frank Newport. http://www.gallup.com/poll/124649/Religious-Intensity-Remains-Powerful-Predictor-Politics.aspx?CSTS=alert.

2. John Halpin, Karl Agne "State of American Political Ideology 2009 A National Study of Values and Beliefs " Center For American Progress, p.14. http://www.americanprogress.org

3. Pew Research Centre, American Mobility, Who Moves, Who Stays put and Where is Home? Updated December 29, 2008 http://pewsocialtrends.org/assets/pdf/Movers-and-Stayers.pdf

4. Ronald Brownstein's The Second Civil War, How Extreme Bipartisanship Has Paralyzed Washington and America was published in 2007.

5. Sam Harris, The End of Faith, Religion: Terror, and The Future of Reason (NY: W.W. Norton & Company, Inc., 2004) 44.

6. Ibid, 45.

7. Peter Berger, (ed.) The Desecularization of the World: Resurgent Religion and World Politics (Grand Rapids, Michigan: Wm. B. Eerdmans Publishing Co. 1999).

8. Bob Harvey, The Future of Religion, Interviews with Christians on the Brink. (Ottawa: Novalis, 2001), 42.

9. Jose Casanova., Public Religions in the Modern World (Chicago: University of Chicago Press, 1994) 11.

10. Alan Wolfe "The Coming Religious Peace," Atlantic Monthly, March 2008.

11. Peter L. Berger, "Secularism in Retreat," The National Interest, (Winter 1996) 47.

12. Pippa Norris and Robert Inglehart, "Gods, Guns and Gays, Supply and demand of religion in the US and Western Europe" http://ksghome.harvard.edu/~pnorris/Acrobat/APSA%202004%20Secularization.pdf, p. 13.

13. Alvin A. Lee and Jean O'Grady, (eds.) Collected Works of Northrop Frye, vol. 4 Northrop Frye on Religion, "The Church: It's Relation to Society," (Toronto: Victoria University, 2000) p. 262.

14. Bernard Lewis and Buntzie Ellis Churchill, Islam: The Religion and the People, (Upper Saddle River, New Jersey: Wharton School Publishing, 2008) 145–150.

15. Fifty-four percent of Americans are now protestant, according to a Gallup Poll published in August, 2009 by Frank Newport Religious Identity: States Differ Widely http://www.gallup.com/poll/122075/Religious-Identity-States-Differ-Widely.aspx?CSTS=alert

16. Peter Berger, "Secularism in Retreat," 4.

17. Thomas L. Friedman, "This Fake News Report is Only Too True" New York Times, October 23, 2005.

CHAPTER 2 –
THE CLASH BETWEEN
SECULARISM AND
MONOTHEISM

> When reason is against man, man will turn against reason
> —David Hume

The primary thesis of *Secular Hope* is that the underlying cause of the modern religious resurgence is the myth of monotheism. By studying monotheism, as opposed to the Reformation, the concerns of believers become easier to articulate in rational terms. Simultaneously, the concerns of secularists can be more clearly addressed because the wall of separation was designed to contain absolute monotheism that threatens all citizens' freedom of conscience. Finally, understanding monotheism significantly improves the possibility of reconciling the Judeo-Christian and Islamic traditions because it starts the discussion from a common point of reference.

The secondary thesis of *Secular Hope* is that America's political crisis is merely a crisis of language.[1] America does not have a constitutional crisis; and it is not engaged in an irreconcilable clash between civilizations. America's only problem is its failure to appreciate the critical difference between *secularization* and *secularism,* which is easiest to understand after a historical review of monotheism.[2] This chapter therefore, first reviews the unique nature of myth, then moves onto the historical development of both monotheism and secularism. It then compares the underlying assumptions of each and concludes by showing why the two concepts are irreconcilable. Chapter Three introduces the solution, secularization.

UNDERSTANDING THE NATURE OF MYTH

Constitutions are *ahistorical* documents in that they must rest on universal truths that can transcend time in order to gain their authority. In this regard, constitutions share the same function as myths—which is why the current clash is between the constitutional objectives of secularism and the myth of monotheism. Understanding myths as critical frameworks of unarticulated assumptions,[3] rather than rationalizations for outdated superstitions, reframes the current political gridlock as a conflict of translation, and not as battles between religious and secular, educated versus ignorant, or even worse, good versus evil. Understanding the modern value in the myth of monotheism is critical to rebuilding the trust necessary to identify and sustain a permanent solution to America's conflicts.

Joseph Campbell, Karen Armstrong and Northrop Frye have all significantly contributed to the academic work that has uncovered the nature and the current social value of myths. The following quotations demonstrate why understanding the nature of myth provides for a more elegant explanation of the recent return to religion than the Secularism Lite thesis or Peter Berger's three explanations. Campbell's first quotation, critiquing a leading psychologist from the 1890s, still applies to today's secularists:

He seems to have had no sense at all of their relevance and importance to inner life, and was confident with the progress and development of science and technology, both magic and religion would ultimately fade away, the ends that they had been thought to serve being better and more surely serviced by science.[4]

Campbell on the primacy of mythical influence on human values:

When we consider ... the psychological character of our species, the most evident distinguishing sign is man's organization of his life according to mythic, and only secondarily economic, aims and laws. Food and drink, reproduction and nest-building, it is true, play formidable roles in the lives no less of men than of chimpanzees. But what of the economics of the Pyramids, the cathedrals of the Middle Ages, Hindus starving to death with edible cattle strolling all around them, or the history of Israel, from the time of Saul until now? If a differentiating feature is to be named, separating human from animal psychology, it is surely this of the subordination in the human sphere of even economics to mythology. [5]

Campbell's quotation exposes fundamentalism as a limitation of mythical thinking. However, it also shows what secularism must create in order to fully usurp the influence of myth:

Now the peoples of all the great civilizations everywhere have been prone to interpret their own symbolic figures literally, and so to regard themselves as favored in a special way, in direct contact with the absolute ... For not only has it always been the way of multitudes to interpret their own symbols literally, but such literally symbolic forms have always been—and still are, in fact—the supports of their civilization, the supports of their moral orders, their cohesion, vitality, and creative powers. [6]

Myth's advantage is that it entertains, while reason must teach, explain, and lecture. Therefore, mythology is more broadly accessible in a way that political philosophy is not. Indeed, the competition can be fierce, because myths can actually impede rational thinking. In the words of Lenn Goodman, a professor of philosophy at Vanderbilt University:

Myth devours category distinctions typical in conceptual thinking. Notoriously, it collapses distinctions of self from other, subject from object, class (tribe, species, kind) from individual, cause from effect, things from names, or wholes from parts-not least in mythic expressions of the experience of the divine. [7]

Because myth does not specify subjects and objects, it can easily encourage self-serving rationalizations to be projected as the will of God, or absolute truth. The longest serving example of this mythical thinking is the myth of the divine right of kings. This circular logic can be summarized as—Henry conquered therefore God willed it to be (might = right), and now that Henry clearly has God's blessing, he can legitimately use violence to preserve God's will (right = might). While this example seems outdated, this type of thinking continues to seduce politicians, executives, and athletes today, who once elected, hired or drafted, believe that they are above the rules. They no longer see themselves as *subject* to the law, or to any promises they have made. This rationalization is summarized in Lord Acton's saying "Power tends to corrupts; and Absolute Power corrupts absolutely". While this is the downside to mythical thinking, the same technique of switching subject/object or cause and effect, can also be used for good reasons, as will be explored later.

With this understanding of myth's strengths and weaknesses, the exact nature of the myth of monotheism which is enjoying a global resurgence today, can be appropriately understood and appreciated. The following historical review reveals the assumptions of monotheism which can be then be compared to the "supporting" assumptions of secularism.

HISTORICAL DEVELOPMENT OF MONOTHEISM

Monotheism is the belief that there is only one God and it is a shared tenet of Judaism, Christianity and Islam. It is not clear whether Judaism was influenced by the monotheism of ancient Egypt or by Zorastrianism during the Babylonian captivity of the sixth century BCE. Indeed, it is not even clear if Moses was truly monotheistic or merely monolaterist (worshipping one god while acknowledging the existence of others). However, what is clear is that today all three religions subscribe to the basic tenets of monotheism; the development of which can be most easily traced in Egyptian history.

In ancient Egypt the first sign of monotheism arose in the god Ptah, the god of the craftsmen. Ptah created eight other gods who were themselves also able to create, but whose creations were still considered to be manifestations of Ptah. It was said that when Ptah spoke, the world came into being. According to G.I.A.D. Draper, in the god Ptah we first "see the idea of an invisible, unknowable God who knows everything."[8] This idea reflects the first tenet of monotheism—that there is one ultimate creator with an objective, universal perspective of the entire world. The world therefore is a cohesive unit, not merely a collection of random events or competing forces.

By 1500 BCE, Amen was referenced in the following line from a hymn "Legitimate Lord, father of the gods, who created man and made all the animals." The phrase "Legitimate Lord, father of the Gods" evidences for the first time that one supreme god was given complete political legitimacy because he was the creator of *all* beings. This hymn shows how political power was derived from metaphysical creative powers and is consistent with the idea of natural law. This orientation is still reflected in the English tradition of the Archbishop of Canterbury conducting the coronation ceremonies of its monarchy, as well in the references to "God" that can be found in most political constitutions. Finally, connecting the creation of the world with political legitimacy instilled the idea that understanding our essential nature is morally relevant.

By 1400 BCE, the first truly monotheistic god appeared as the Egyptian Sun god Aten. He was identified as "the Lord of the Universe and the distant lands" and clearly commanded the elimination of all other gods during the reign of Akhenaten between 1370-50 BCE.[9] This imperial aspect of monotheism, which commands an exclusive political commitment, is the problematic aspect of monotheism.

The final step in the full development of monotheism, according to Draper, is represented in the personalized nature of the Jewish monotheistic god Yahweh, as a god of each individual, not just the Israelite people.[10] This is an extension of the concept of God being the creator of all human beings. A key aspect of all three monotheist religions is that God has a personal interest in every individual's well-being. This aspect of monotheism has been expressed recently in more modern language, where individuals become the subject of the concept. Harvey Cox in his recent book *The Future of Faith* defined religion, or more specifically faith, as our unique approaches to the mystery of human nature.[11]

In summary, the central tenet of monotheism is that Yahweh/God/Allah is a metaphor for a universal moral truth. In addition to the direct references to the highest truth in religious scripture, the very notion of God's power and authority lies in the fact that he/she sees and understands everything and therefore cannot be lied to. Hence, ultimate justice can only be delivered by one who sees the whole truth. This is not to suggest that Yahweh/God/Allah is *only* a metaphor for truth, but rather that for the purposes of understanding secularization, it is necessary to agree that a critical aspect of the monotheistic concept of God is a reference to an objective universal moral truth. The final aspect of this objective truth is that it concerns our essential human nature, therein serving as a legitimating source of political power, much like the concept of natural law.

Monotheism is more than just a statement on the number of gods that may exist—it is worthy of the term *mythos*, because in the words of Joseph Campbell, it provides the "supports of our civilization, moral orders, cohesion, vitality, and creative powers". Monotheism provides the structural tension underlying all three monotheistic religions which is that one God created the incredible diversity of all human beings. In this regard, monotheism is no different than a constitution that claims universal moral authority over a culturally pluralistic society. Ironically, the mythos monotheism becomes more relevant in a globalized society, not less.

In the West, legal moral reasoning has recently evolved separately from religious morality, but both moral codes share monotheism's objective of enunciating laws that are universally applicable. The following is a list of the assumptions contained in the myth of monotheism which can then be compared with those contained in variations of secularism.

DEFINING MONOTHEISM AND MONOTRUISM

Based on the preceding historical review, monotheism can be summarized with the following assumptions. This definition represents an absolute form of monotheism, that few now practice, but it is easiest to start with the purest form in order to understand the framework of assumptions.

1. There is an objective, universal truth regarding human nature (monotruism) that underlies beliefs about right and wrong (morality);

2. Religion is the only means of understanding that universal moral truth;

3. Only one religion is the legitimate means of understanding moral truth.

When considering the success of the traditional secularization theory, it was correct in essentially predicting the demise of the second and third of monotheism's assumptions–that religion, and one religion in particular, is the exclusive path to universal truth. For most of the world, at issue now is the question of whether we should proceed with an understanding that there is one objective truth worth pursuing politically, or should we be content with multiple versions of truth.

The residual value in the myth of monotheism, that is critical to understanding the following discussion on secularism, may be called monotruism. While this concept is close to the idea of monism (all matter is a unified whole) or universalism (all people will be saved) it is narrower in that it merely asserts that an objective truth regarding human nature exists, and underlies concepts of right and wrong ways to treat each other. Now secularism may be explained as variations on each of monotheism's three dimensions. And similarly, secularism is best understood by reviewing its developmental history.

HISTORICAL DEVELOPMENT OF SECULARISM

The term *secular* covers a great variety of constitutional models—but their common characteristic is their objective of divesting religion of its exclusive moral authority. Secular governments, which have only existed in the last three hundred years, of our five thousand years of human civilization, can be distinguished as those whose political decision makers receive their legitimacy from rational theories of governance. Prior to this time, monarchies and institutional churches co-ruled on the theological premise of the divine right to rule. At its most basic level, secular means that political authority vests on rational, not theological grounds.

The meaning of the term *secularism* has evolved significantly as the role of religion has changed in society. Secularism was first coined by George Holyoake in 1851 but quickly altered by Charles Bradlaugh in 1856, who co-founded the National Secular Society in England. Attempts to keep up with its meaning have resulted in the use of relative descriptors such as hard/soft, open/restrictive, radical/non-radical. These descriptors, however, have only compounded the confusion because the original point of reference varies by country and time.

As more meaningful alternatives, Romantic Secularism, Rational Secularism and Postmodern Secularism are proposed because they reference the assumptions that put them at odds with monotheism as well as being grounded in the evolution of term. Just as with the term monotheism, it is helpful to understand the developmental history of the term *secularism* because more specific definitions create more opportunities for compromise. The chart located in *Appendix I Comparing Assumptions* allows for easier comparisons between monotheism and each of the different forms of secularism.

When reason was first advanced as an alternative source of moral authority, few were convinced that humans could actually reason objectively because the predominant view at the time was that humans were naturally selfish. This position was rationally argued by Thomas Hobbes (1588-1689), but was more widely accepted on the basis of the theological notion of original sin. Consequently, Enlightenment thinkers like Locke (1632-1704) and Voltaire (1694-1778) were not immediately successful in having their ideas implemented.

It first took Jean-Jacques Rousseau's (1712-1778) Romantic Movement to convince the West that human nature was essentially good before humans would be trusted with the independent ability to reason and vote. Rousseau, as the poet's philosopher, believed that without oppressive institutions, humans were naturally moderate and compassionate and therefore could be relied upon to use their own sentiments and ability to reason to effectively govern themselves. Rousseau's arguments were widely and readily accepted and thus played a critical role in the political de-establishment of both the church and monarchy in France and America.

Romanticism paved the way for both reason and sentiment to flourish, but it was sentiment that played the leading role. Thomas Paine's infamous pamphlet "Common Sense" was not entitled "Learned Reason" and even he was not an atheist. Neither was Jefferson.[12] Nor was he an advocate of judicial supremacy as many of today's secularists would like to believe. In Jefferson's view the people were clearly the final arbiters of all political conflicts. With the new American constitution, it was the "common sense" of the people that usurped moral authority from the mutually entrenching monarchy and institutional churches.

The important point is that in order to understand the history of secularism, it is necessary to reframe politics not as a two-sided tug of war between reason and religion, but rather like the three legged stool that keeps tipping over. Truth is a trinity of reason (mind), personal experiences and feelings (body) and religion (spirit). Truth is a trinity because each has their respective strengths and weaknesses. Romantic Secularism, tried to balance all three, and was the first response to the tyranny that often resulted from granting monarchs the absolute right to rule.

ROMANTIC SECULARISM

Romantic Secularism is based on a social contract that proposes that the highest political values are individual freedom and equality. Romantic Secularism respects the role of reason and religion in forming one's beliefs, but really champions the individual and their right to their own experiences. Hence the liberal democracies of Romantic Secularism always ensure that individual human rights are constitutionally entrenched. The American Constitution was the first expression of Romantic Secularism. Its most defining secular feature is the constitutional wall that separates the private realm of beliefs or spirituality from the public, material world of actions so that individual freedom of conscience would always be protected.

Romantic Secularism was not in direct conflict with monotheism because the wall of separation allowed monotruism (belief in one moral truth for all) to be practiced by both church and state, but only within their respective jurisdictions. By separating the institutions of church and state, American citizens were the first to gain the unprecedented power to choose both their religious beliefs and their governments. Romantic Secularism can be expressed in the following assumptions:

1. There are two moral universes: one public and one private;

2. Each citizen is sufficiently free to have their own personal experiences, religious beliefs and reasoning; and through the right to vote is allowed to contribute to the determination of the universal moral truth in the public realm;

3. Governments are to remain neutral with regard to private beliefs in order to protect equality and freedom of religion and conscience.

Romantic Secularism is appropriately titled for three reasons. Firstly, it was rationalized on the belief that *individuals* using their experiences and sentiments were better trusted than institutional clergy or bureaucrats, to arrive at moral conclusions. Secondly, it reflected the sentimental belief that the private and public realms could co-exist without conflict. For some this belief rested on the assumption that religious values would remain consistent with the universal moral truth as rationally determined by the political system. This opinion was expressed by John Adams: "The substance and essence of Christianity, as I understand it, is eternal and unchangeable, and will bear examination forever."[13]

Finally, it was a romantic notion in the sense that it was only a theoretical compromise. Few truly gave up believing in a universal truth that covered both sides of the wall of separation. Both sides considered it a practical, temporary compromise that would disappear as their version truth eventually converted the other. For the secularist, this meant that secularization would eventually render religious beliefs obsolete. For the religious, it meant that eventually God's moral truth would triumph either in the afterlife or here on earth through universal acceptance of Christianity. This is the unifying power of metaphor at work; the ability to gloss over inconsequential differences, in order to build common ground.

All things considered, the private/public jurisdictional wall did work very well for over two hundred years. This was because for the most part churches had no interest in the *Bees Keeper Act* and the state had no interest in declaring saints. Most importantly, where there was overlapping interest; there was consistency—murder and theft are both sins and crimes.

Same-sex marriage is proving to be a serious constitutional problem because the jurisdictional rules do not work with this issue. Marriage does not fall neatly into either private or public classifications, because marriage has both spiritual and material aspects and consequences. The definition of marriage demonstrates how the theoretical line between public and private can break down. Consider the following quotation from an article entitled "Celebrating marriage across Canada" that illustrates the private and public nature of marriage:

> Leigh Cousins, who proposed to Mandy Randhawa in October after 11 years of dating, says their marriage is not only a personal affair but a social and political statement to show their hopes and dreams are no different than other couples. "There is something very important and sacred about being public about it," says Randhawa. "For me it's a celebration of my love and my choices and my life as an individual."[14]

Unfortunately, when the private/public line breaks down, and protected freedoms clash with equality rights, Romantic Secularism has no way to declare a winner by appealing to a higher value. In Canada, this legal conundrum was explored in a 2005 article in Ontario's *Lawyers Gazette:*[15]

> While courts have been expanding equality rights to cover a range of different types of discrimination not specifically set out in Section 15, the real test to its mettle will come when courts are forced to stack it up against other protected rights.

Beverley Baines, a law professor at Queen's University, was quoted in the same article:

> "However, I don't think we fully grasped the threat that major religion – Christianity, Islam and Judaism – would pose for woman's equality rights..." Baines says she was "astounded to learn

that 75–90% of marriages in Canada involved
some form of religious auspices." She thinks
"churches should get out of the marriage business"
otherwise it will be difficult to keep civil and
religious regulation of marriage separate. While
the Supreme Court insists there is no hierarchy of
rights in the Charter, there is no "clear foundation
to sustain it" she says.

The second reason for today's crisis is that there is a clear moral
conflict between the principles underlying liberal democracies
and most traditional religions because their scriptures are quite
explicit on the heterosexual nature of marriage. Finally, all the
major religions are consistent on the issue (even Buddhism as
expressed by the Dalai Lama) making political majorities much
easier to obtain. Even abortion did not have the power to unite
the religious community politically; therefore this is a significant
development in the history of Romantic Secularism.

Across the United States, courts have not found traction
in resolving the same-sex marriage debate because, just like
the Canadian Constitution, the American Constitution has no
principled way to settle a conflict between equality rights and
freedom of religion. Acknowledging that there is no higher
principle to break the tie, David Blankenhorn and Jonathan
Rauch, arch-enemies on the same-sex marriage issue, wrote the
following warning in 2009 as an appeal for compromise:

> In all sharp moral disagreements, maximalism is
> the constant temptation. People dig in, positions
> harden and we tend to convince ourselves that
> our opponents are not only wrong-headed but
> also malicious and acting in bad faith. In such
> conflicts, it can seem not only difficult but wrong
> to compromise on a core belief. But clinging
> to extremes can also be quite dangerous, a
> scorched-earth debate, pitting what some regard

as a nonnegotiable religious freedom against what others regard as a nonnegotiable human right, would do great harm to our civil society. When a reasonable accommodation on a tough issue seems possible, both sides should have the courage to explore it. [16]

As of March 2010, American states continued to be split on same-sex marriage, and if the current trend of Americans settling in like-minded communities continues, then federalism is at risk. The practical limitations of the theory behind the separation of church and state will only become more obvious as unforeseen consequences arising from conflicts between woman's issues, reproductive technologies, and bioethics are litigated. In summary, same-sex marriage is the issue that has created a constitutional crisis for Romantic Secularism because:

1. Marriage is a public announcement of a private commitment with both public (property) and private (spiritual) implications, making a mockery of the private/public distinction necessary for the smooth functioning of Romantic Secularism;

2. All traditional religions are consistent on the matter making a majority easier to achieve;

3. Splitting marriage into its spiritual (religious marriage) and material aspects (secular civil unions) still does not offer the Gay, Lesbian, Bisexual, and Transgender (GLBT) community the full acceptance and feelings of equality they are seeking;

4. As Hobbes first articulated, monotheistic religions teach a higher allegiance to their religion over state authority, creating a profound crisis where the two conflict;

5. Both sides have constitutionally-protected rights at stake, and each believes the other side is betraying the spirit of the secular constitution, rather than acknowledging the limits of the constitution.

The consequence is that individual citizens drift to morally consistent communities, rather than separate their political and spiritual morality. Next in the history of secularism is Rational Secularism, which has also played a significant, if indirect, role in American and international politics.

RATIONAL SECULARISM

Rational Secularism asserts the untouchable supremacy of reason above all other forms of knowledge. Communism is an example of Rational Secularism and is based on the theory that economic equality is the only foundation for true human freedom. It was originally proposed by Karl Marx and its dogmatic nature is best expressed by this quotation of his "The meaning of peace is the absence of opposition to socialism."

Rational Secularism does not believe that reason and religion should be reconciled by citizens, or anyone else, because religion is only useful for keeping workers unconscious of, and therefore satisfied with, their economic slavery. Further, communism does not believe that citizens should reconcile their personal experiences with reason, because only a select group of intellectuals were capable of resisting the temptation to own private property—the source of all inequality. Consequently, under communist regimes, both religion and human rights are legitimately suppressed by law. Rational Secularism is most similar to Absolute Monotheism as both must control education, the flow of information, freedom of association and non-government organizations in order to be successful. This similarity is easiest to appreciate by comparing the three assumptions of Rational Secularism with Absolute Monotheism:

1. There is only one universal moral truth;

2. *Reason*, as articulated by proletariat dictatorship, is the only legitimate path to a universal truth and freedom;

3. Proletariat reasoning based on the assumption that establishing equality is the only legitimate path to universal truth and freedom.

As history has shown, Soviet Communism was defeated on each level of commitment:

1. There was more than one truth. No one could live with the truth of communism, least of all its leaders. George Orwell said it best in *Animal Farm*: "All animals are created equal, but some are more equal than others";

2. The resilience of religious beliefs, despite seriously weakened Churches, suggests the truth in revelation to be at least as compelling, if not superior to the rational values of communism;

3. Many citizens continually risked their lives to live in freedom, providing contrary empirical evidence to the theory that equality was the best path to freedom.

Reaction to monotheism's religious dogma (unquestionable truths) set off a chain of equally dogmatic rational claims, and hence producing equally violent and abusive regimes. Monotheism was first countered by Communism, which was then itself challenged by the even more dogmatic Axis Powers of WWII. The Anti-Comintern Pact signed by Germany and

Japan in 1936, and Italy in 1937 was designed to counter to the absolute truth claims of Communism:

> Recognizing that the aim of the Communist International, known as the Comintern, is to disintegrate and subdue existing States by all the means at its command; convinced that the toleration of interference by the Communist International in the internal affairs of the nations not only endangers their internal peace and social well-being, but is also a menace to the peace of the world desirous of co-operating in the defense against Communist subversive activities.

Countering the monotruism of Marxism, on the basis of the supremacy of the Aryan race, the Nazi regime quickly became the most repugnant form of Rational Secularism for murdering between 11-17 million people (Jewish, homosexual, disabled, Polish, Romani, Soviet, Marxist, clergy, and intellectual) on the common rationale that by even existing, they challenged the truth of German superiority or Hitler's right to absolute rule. Hitler's rationalization was that he could prove Aryan superiority if he could just first eliminate all these 'obstacles'. The American equivalent can be found in the white nationalism advocated by the Ku Klux Klan.

Legitimate concerns with monotruistic claims include how easily they may be abused by political rhetoric that preys on feelings of inferiority and despair. Dogmatists are those who subscribe exclusively to either reason or religion as the only means of knowing truth, with a simultaneous commitment to one absolute truth. Dogmatists will insist upon the universality of their version of truth by *cynically* dismissing dissenters as morally deficient, blasphemous, uneducated, too vulnerable to admit the reality of their own situations, opiate-addicted or evil, therein justifying violence or oppression in the name of progress, equality, nationalism, God, peace, or civilization. Rational Secularism is especially prone to fail when it advances a theory of human nature that is only validated by the experiences of a limited population, the extreme example being a dictator basing his reasoning solely on his own subjective desires and experiences.

The dogmatic forms of both Absolute Monotheism and Rational Secularism have justified the most horrible wars to "prove" their universal claims. However, we must remain vigilant against milder forms. Rational Secularism has re-emerged with the new atheists of Sam Harris, Richard Dawkins and Christopher Hitchens. The new atheists see religion as irreconcilable with moral truth, fundamentally flawed and nothing but an obstacle to peace. New atheists would limit the freedom of conscience/ religion if they had a significant political following. Once again this *defensive* movement is responding to the violence of absolute monotheists—but it is critical not to make the same mistakes as the last set of Rational Secularists. This can be done by trying to understand the positive allure of monotheism, while remaining wary of its violent potential. This brings us to Postmodern Secularism which tries to avoid the danger of absolute truth claims by constitutionalizing diversity.

POSTMODERN SECULARISM

Postmodern Secularism is heavily influenced by the academic work that evolved in response to the horrors of the Nazi concentration camps of the 1930's and 40's as well as the Soviet human right abuses that were exposed in the 1980's. It is also simultaneously responding to increased pressure to expand the public sphere in which religious beliefs can play a legitimate role. The United Nations (UN), Canada and the European Union (EU) all adopted their secular commitment to human rights following WWII (the UN in 1948, Canada in 1982, and the EU in 2000). Therefore each adopted this form of secularism which share variations of the Preamble contained in the 1948 UN Declaration on Human Rights:

Whereas recognition of the inherent dignity and
of the equal and inalienable rights of all members
of the human family is the foundation of freedom,
justice and peace in the world,

Whereas disregard and contempt for human
rights have resulted in barbarous acts which have
outraged the conscience of mankind, and the
advent of a world in which human beings shall
enjoy freedom of speech and belief and freedom
from fear and want has been proclaimed as the
highest aspiration of the common people,

Whereas it is essential, if man is not to be
compelled to have recourse, as a last resort, to
rebellion against tyranny and oppression, that
human rights should be protected by the rule of
law...[17]

Postmodern Secularism goes further than Romantic
Secularism's neutrality on spiritual beliefs by elevating human
dignity, equality, tolerance, and diversity of cultures, as the
highest political values, even above freedom. The assumptions of
Postmodern Secularism follow this line of reasoning:

1. There is no universal truth regarding human
    nature that underlies morality;

2. Personal experiences, religion and reasoning
    are all valid paths to multiple truths, but only
    to the point that they are tolerant of other's
    experiences;

3. The highest common moral truth is pluralism,
    tolerance and equality of self-respect.

There are four ways for Romantic Secularism to evolve into
Postmodern Secularism. One way is to erase the jurisdictional

boundaries that enforce state neutrality by settling disputes between freedom of religion and equality rights in favor of ensuring diversity. A second method is to encourage the state to use its powers to restrict freedoms when feelings of self-respect, not just physical or financial harm is caused. This is justified on the basis that it is not enough for the state to ensure that everyone is equally free to express and live out their own beliefs, but rather states should ensure that minorities *feel* that their beliefs are equally respected so that they can live with equal dignity. A third strategy is often required to overrule majority votes in order to enforce tolerance, especially when countering religiously informed beliefs. Finally, seeking to reconcile American rights with international human rights covenants would also cause America's Romantic Secularism to morph into Postmodern Secularism.

While Postmodern Secularism effectively guards against the abuses of Rational Secularists and Absolute Monotheists, and addresses the short-comings of Romantic Secularism, there are three serious problems with it. The common thread of which is that Postmodern Secularism is at irreconcilable odds with monotheism and is causing the global religious resurgence. Many mild monotheists have a problem seeing this conflict because they see the essence of their religions as promoting tolerance and compassion. Hopefully, the following reasons will help them understand.

1. Rejects Monotruism

While claiming to respect diversity, Postmodern Secularism cannot accommodate monotheists (over 80% of Americans).[18] However, the rejection is not due to the imperial or tyrannical aspects of monotheism as contained in the second and third assumptions, but rather the first philosophical assumption of monotheism, monotruism. Postmodern Secularism does not tolerate monotruism because in postmodern societies there is no higher truth than tolerance, plurality and equality. This line of thinking makes the personal or subjective experience of truth, the highest form of truth. On specific issues, particularly those related to sexuality, this rationale seems justified but it has far-reaching consequences that are causing havoc in other areas of morality, where trust is critical.

The historical event that prompted the majority of Americans to trade reason in for religion demonstrates the importance of monotruism's commitment to objective truth that underlies trust. In 1998, President Bill Clinton's indiscretions with Monica Lewinsky made their way into the public sphere and marked the end of the paved road for unfettered liberalism in the United States. When President Clinton tried to get away with his subjective definition of "I did not have sexual relations with that woman"; the majority of Americans reacted strongly by voting in the opposite bias. Allegiance to objective truth is the basis of security in all personal, business and governmental relationships. It is the foundation of morality; it is not its enemy.

2. REJECTS THE EXPERIENCES OF THE MAJORITY

It is easy to justify Postmodern Secularism when the conflict is pitched as a David and Goliath battle between the personal dignity of a homosexual versus the intolerant, 3,000 year old scripture condemning him to death. However, it should be considered that members of the religious right may also have *personal experiences* that they understandably do not wish to discuss publicly, but contradict the theory of human nature articulated by human rights cases that granted protection of homosexual rights. Members of the religious right may be attracted to their religions, not out of passive inheritance, economic vulnerability, or hatred/fear of homosexuals but rather because their churches articulate, and support, a concept of human sexuality that most closely mirrors their *own* personal experiences and psychological needs.

While it is agreed that most, if not all, homosexuals *do not* have a choice with regard to their sexuality, there is plenty of evidence to show that many heterosexuals *do* experience a choice with regard to their sexuality. A recent large study showed that 25% of junior and high school students were confused over their sexuality, even when the heterosexual category was qualified as *predominately* heterosexual. However the vast majority of the confused students, with time and experience, eventually realized a predominantly heterosexual identity, while less than 2% identified as exclusively homosexual or bi-sexual.[19]

As the Kinsey Report infamously argued over sixty years ago, the far more common experience of sexual orientation is to experience a choice especially during adolescence and then to identify as predominantly, but not exclusively, heterosexual as an adult. While it can be argued that one's *degree* of choice may be fixed after adolescence, clearly there is a choice to be made if one wants to enter into a monogamous marriage for life. Monogamous marriages with children remain the ideal form of relationships therefore choices, with long-term and wide-spread moral implications, do need to be made. Further, the now visible gay community in the public sphere continually reminds them of this choice, and hence their attraction to private institutions that acknowledge and support them in their choice. One does not have to be a Freudian to see how this would explain homophobia and why the religious right is claiming that same-sex marriage affects the stability of their families.

It is critical to understand the nuanced nature of this argument. Homosexuals, as human beings and citizens, are fully deserving of respect and protection as guaranteed by civil/human rights. That issue thankfully is largely past the need for further discussion. Further, given their higher suicide rates, obviously homosexuals rarely experience having a degree of choice with regard to their sexuality. However, there are many ways for this to still be true, but not necessarily be a universal attribute of human nature.

Religious beliefs may be a shield against a secular theory of human nature that contradicts believers own personal experiences and choices. Understandably, the judgmental aspect of religious support is troubling: but why go so far as to deny the element of choice for others? The implications of implying that *nobody* has a choice with regard to their sexuality, albeit for the compassionate reasons of trying to assist homosexuals with accepting their unique identities, needs to be re-considered. To deprive others of any choices they may have, was not the motivation of the GLBT community but it is having this effect.

It is suggested that the reason for this unfortunate conflict is that the inflexible legal moral code, only granted human rights protection on the basis of "immutable" characteristics, forcing this strategy on the GLBT and their advocates. While it has the right effect for the gay community, the underlying premise is wrong and is resulting in an irreconcilable fight over human nature and morality that is causing a counter-resurgence of hyper-masculinity and monotheism. It is important to stress that that the gay community deserves human right protection; but that an inflexible legal test forced an exaggerated truth claim.

3. SIBLING SOCIETY

That some members of the GLBT community even *want* religiously blessed marriages in a secular age raises the most compelling aspect of monotheism. When monotheism is considered mythically, meaning the subject and object are reversed, the notion that there is only one God who created all human beings, allows every individual to conclude "I *must* belong". When multiple Gods/universes/truths become the philosophical foundation for a society, the "must" disappears. Now individuals must make the decision of where to belong, creating in most people a level of existential angst that is very difficult to endure.

The Postmodern equivalent of monotheism's universal claim was articulated as the "inherent dignity of all members of the human family". While this concept ensures equal access to civil rights, it falls well short of providing the full psychological/ spiritual comfort provided by monotruism's assumption of a universal truth regarding human nature. Postmodern Secularism can protect but it cannot comfort.

The most detrimental aspect of losing the commitment to objective truth is that it turns citizens into siblings without parents, where nobody is wiser than anyone else.[20] This explains why the GLBT community is seeking monotheistic equality in the definition of marriage, not just civil equality. They are seeking universal respect and acknowledgement, not just tolerance. Unfortunately, it is impossible for the state to provide. The state can only write and enforce laws, it cannot create community.

This review of secularism does not come to a promising conclusion: neither Romantic nor Postmodern Secularism, are viable options to significant portions of America. Is there a way out of these profound conflicts? It's hard to concentrate as the laughter of the Greek gods grows louder by the day. However, there are three promising clues left to explore: i) the taunting maxim "Know Thyself" inscribed in the Temple of Apollo at Delphi and reiterated by John Adams in his quotation:

> Every Species of these Christians would persecute Deists, as [much] as either Sect would persecute another, if it had unchecked and unbalanced Power. Nay, the Deists would persecute Christians, and Atheists would persecute Deists, with as unrelenting Cruelty, as any Christians would prosecute them or one another. *Know Thyself, Human Nature!*[21] [Emphasis added].

The second is Harvey Cox's 1965 warning not to lose the distinction between secularism and secularization, and the third lies in Northrop Frye's *The Great Code*. Hopefully, it's not too late to heed their advice.

NOTES

1. Lee and O'Grady (eds.) Frye on Religion, 177; Habermas, Jurgen Religion and Rationality, 22.

2. Secularism and Secularization are terms that have been interpreted in a variety of ways. While Secular Hope explores these definitions in great detail throughout Chapters Two and Three, they are also easily referenced in the Glossary located after Appendix I.

3. For those interested in this fascinating line of study, Northrop Frye's 1990 book Words with Power, Being A Second Study of The Bible and Literature is highly recommended as is the work of Lenn E. Goodman.

4. Joseph Campbell, Myths to Live By (NY: Penguin Compass, 1972) 13.

5. Ibid, 22.

6. Ibid, 10.

7. L. E. Goodman, The God of Abraham (NY: Oxford University Press, 1996) 6.

8. "The Historical Background on the Concept of Monotheism" found in The Concept of Monotheism in Islam and Christianity, Ed. Kochler, Hans, Wilhelm Braumuller A1092-Wien, Austria, p. 34.

9. Ibid, 35.

10. Ibid, 36.

11. Harvey Cox, The Future of Hope, (NY: Harper Collins, 2009) 37.

12. Jefferson was a Deist; he believed that God exists but that he does not intervene in the world.

13. J.F. Adams, (ed.) The Works of John Adams, vols. 10 (Boston: Little & Brown, 1850-56) 415-416.

14. "Celebrating marriage across Canada", Metro News Services Tuesday June 23, 2009.

15. Lawyers Gazette Fall/Winter 2005, p. 11 published by the Law Society of Upper Canada.

16. New York Times, February 22, 2009. Sunday Opinion Week in Review, 11.

17. http://www.un.org/en/documents/udhr/

18. Pew Forum 2007 study found at http://religions.pewforum.org/pdf/report-religious-landscape-study-full.pdf.

19. In a large, study of junior and senior high school students in the late 1980s that measured sexual fantasy, emotional attraction, and sexual behavior, more than 25% of 12-year-olds were uncertain about their sexual orientation. This was even when the category of "predominantly heterosexual" was offered. This uncertainty decreased, with time and increasing sexual experience to 5% of 18-year-olds. Only 1.1% reported themselves as predominantly homosexual or bisexual. "Demography of sexual orientation in adolescents" Pediatrics 1992; 89: 714 –721.

20. Robert Bly's book The Sibling Society, argues that today we have no elders, no children, no past, no future.

21. John Witte Jr. "A most Mild and Equitable Establishment of Religion" John Adams and the Massachusetts Experiment",

in Religion in the New Republic, ed. James H. Hutson, (ed.), (Lanthan MD: Rowman and Littlefield Publishers, Inc., 2000) p.3-4.

CHAPTER 3 –
SECULARIZING THE
PARABLE OF HOPE

> Hope is that virtue that sees the past and the present in light
> of a future horizon
> —Harvey Cox

THE GREAT CODE

The beauty, magic and enduring nature of religion is found in the hope and cohesive meaning it provides, especially during repetitive conflict that can give rise to despair. Now that secularism's irreversible march towards modernity has fragmented into warring factions of itself, a new narrative is required. While this tenacious characteristic of religion has eluded secularism, one scholar discovered it in the literary structure of myths.

Northrop Frye was a humanist literary critic who, in addition to studying the language of myth, was an expert in the Judeo-Christian scriptures. Frye's work provides us with the literary structure, or narrative, of all biblical myths, which he called *The Great Code*. Given that it is the myth of monotheism that is causing the resurgence, it is suggested that the mythical view of time and progress is considered as an alternative to secularism's vision of unlimited linear progress.

Northrop Frye's Great Code has the power to secularize hope by showing us where we have been, where we are now and where we can all agree is the best place to head. While Frye based his work on the Bible, it is suggested that because his findings speak more to the structure of myths, rather than to their content, the Great Code has universal applicability. Further, because the Qur'ân acknowledges the validity of the Judeo-Christian scriptures, it is hoped that this mythical structure, or ahistorical way of looking at history, is also compelling to Muslims.

Frye's study of the old and new testaments as literature revealed a ubiquitous U-shaped plot, or mythos:

> The historical narrative in the Bible is not really a history but a mythos or narrative principle on which historical incidents are strung. We soon realize that we are being told the same story over and over again, and that this story is U shaped. Israel starts in a condition of relative peace, independence, and prosperity, disobeys or forsakes its God, meets with disaster, plunges into humiliation, slavery, and exile, and then a God-appointed redeemer starts it on the way back to its original state.

> This U shaped mythos of fall into bondage and redemption to freedom is not confined to the historical narrative: the entire Christian Bible is enclosed by the Story of Adam, who loses the tree and water of life on the first page of Genesis and gets them back on the last page of Revelation. We find the same pattern in the story of Job—who loses and regains all he has, and in the parable of the Prodigal Son—which incidentally is the

only version in which the protagonist himself determines the point of his return.

It is a mythos closely related to that of a comedy in literature with the same pattern of descent into threatening or actual complications reversed by some providential redemption. Directly opposed to it, and forming the background against it, is the mythos of the recurring rise and fall of heathen empires. The vision is tragic and ironic: the social unit, whatever it is, first rises and then falls, forming an inverted U shape like that of a hero's role in a tragedy.[1]

Frye stated that *real progress* comes from recognizing and applying this plot to current political situations because the Bible was written in mythical language so as to be ahistorical:

The real step forward comes when we see that the entire Biblical vision, from Genesis to Revelation (or Chronicles in Judaism), may be spiritually present in every particular event, and may be in fact the genuine form of that event.[2]

The open U is the truly monotheistic way to look at history—distinct from both the closed Greek circle and modernity's straight line of progress. The U-shape incorporates the best of the ancient and modern views of history. The political power in the U-shaped plot rests in its capacity to culturally transcend the destructive power of traditional monotheism through the first stage of secularization (descent) and then unify the monotheistic religions through the second stage (ascent). Frye points out the hopeful nature of the U-shaped plot:

It looks as though it were the power to *go beyond history* that provides the energy for a new historical cycle: in any case, the U-shaped pattern never turns into a closed circle, with the end exactly identical with the beginning.[3] [Emphasis added]

Now Harvey Cox's distinction between secularization and secularism will be easier to appreciate because it can be visually placed on monotheism's U shaped plot of history.

REVIVING THE SECULARIZATION THEORY

In his best-selling book *The Secular City,* Harvey Cox made a critical distinction between secularism as an ideology and the process of secularization. Ideology equates one form of knowledge with truth; while secularization is the process of reconciling all three means of knowing truth. Unfortunately, that warning has gone unheeded, both academically and in the popular culture. Cox's distinction reads:

> More recently, secularization has been used to describe a process on the cultural level which is parallel to the political one.... Secularization *implies a historical process*, almost certainly irreversible, in which society and culture are delivered from ...religious control and closed metaphysical world-views. We have argued that it is basically a liberating development.

> Secularism on the other hand, is the name for an ideology, a new closed world-view which functions very much like a new religion. While secularization finds its roots in the biblical faith itself and is to some extent an authentic outcome of the impact of biblical faith on Western history, this is not the case with secularism. Like any other ism, it menaces openness and freedom that secularization has produced; it must therefore be watched carefully to prevent its becoming

the ideology of a new establishment. It must be especially checked where it pretends not to be a world-view but nonetheless seeks to impose its ideology through the organs of the state.[4] [Emphasis added].

While these quotations are a bit cryptic, Cox is warning against Postmodern Secularism, which claims to be a universal world-view but must use the organs of the state to enforce this "world-view". Cox's definition of secularization is easier to appreciate when viewed through the three familiar assumptions of monotheism already discussed:

1. There is a universal moral truth, and

2. Reason, religion and personal experiences are all valid paths to the universal truth of human nature.

3. Individuals are responsible for reconciling these forms of knowledge and contributing to a universal understanding of truth through political participation.

Secularization is not the passive discarding of superstitious beliefs, but rather the active process by which individual citizens validate or reject legal changes, through political participation. Because religious morality was mixed with legal morality in the British common law that America inherited, American courts took time to fully remove it. Each decision, however, was publicly assessed by citizens in the context of real-life conflicts. Cultural secularization is not simply a lagging process where religious values are automatically replaced by secular values determined by the courts. It is a democratic indicator of the relative success of the rational legal moral codes over religious moral codes; of logos over mythos.

Cultural secularization is the process of diminishing the moral influence of religion on individuals, but only to the degree that the rational legal system is able to provide an adequate substitute to religious morality. Using this interactive definition, secularization is not dead, but rather is alive and well, especially in America. Secularization is a complete commitment to democratic principles.

Secularization's interactive definition explains why there is a religious resurgence and not a linear decline in religious beliefs. It also explains that when a religion loses its moral authority in a culture, it empowers individuals to develop, trust and rely upon other forms of knowledge, such as reasoning and personal experience. These other forms are also necessary to advance economic objectives, therein explaining the correlation between economic prosperity and secularization. However, there are limits to rational progress and religious or spiritual knowledge may resurface to balance the society that is losing its commitment to secularization by slipping into secular ideology.

Secularization is also the historical narrative of monotheism. The U-shaped mythos always commences with a simple state of unity, and then descends into fragmentation, conflict, and despair before winding back upward toward a complex state of unity that recognizes and accommodates the underlying diversity it just discovered. Applying *The Great Code* of Hope to the history of monotheism, we can see that we are currently somewhere on the bottom of the U, in a state of irreconcilable differences. But the current religious resurgence is not about a return to simple monotheism, but is, rather, a quest to move past secularism. It represents hope for a day where the wall of separation is no longer necessary because church and state are fully reconciled in the heart of every citizen. Secularization is monotheism secularizing into monotruism through a U-shaped plot. A full review of this historical journey is provided in Appendix II – Monotheism's Historical Plot of Hope.

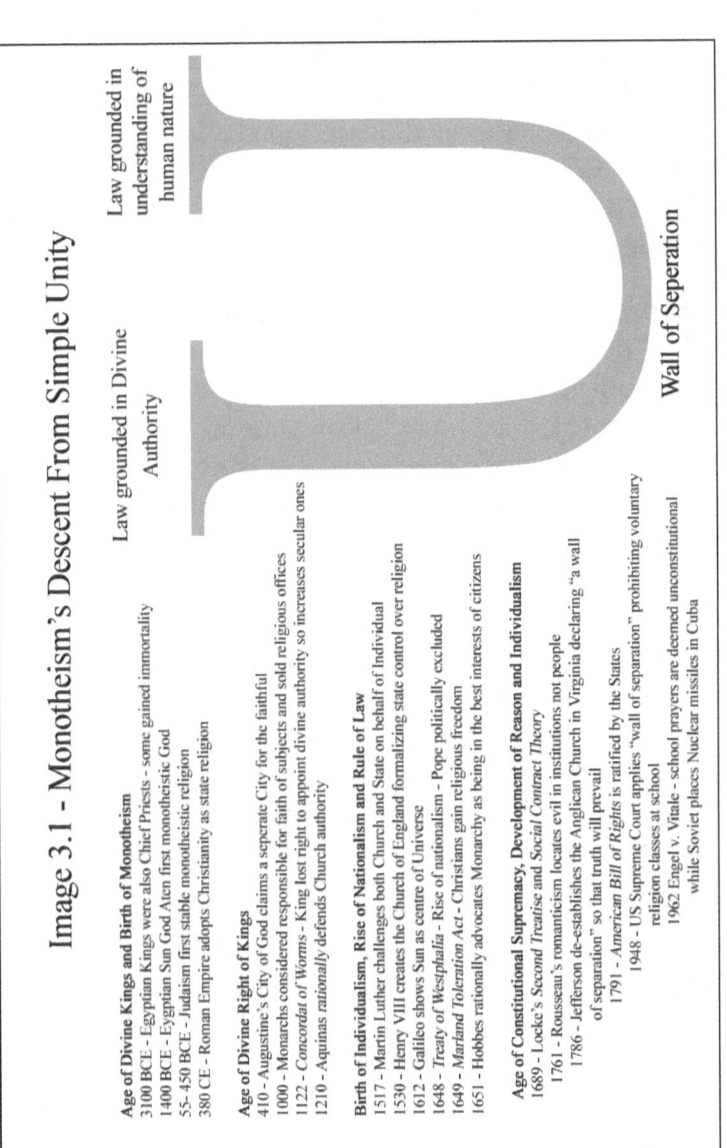

Monotheism's descent from Simple Unity

The metaphoric wall is a critical part of Western history which needs to remain until religious myths are fully secularized because it provides legal protection to ensure that everyone is sufficiently free to reconcile their mind, bodies and souls. However, the wall has a much better chance of surviving politically, today, if it is justified on the basis of secularization, and not with the demands of secularism. The wall of separation should not become another false idol. Draper summarized the similarities of the three monotheistic religions:

> Between the three religions there is a distinct line of paternity in relation to the concept of monotheism. In each of these three religions it is accepted that monotheism came to man by way of a Divine Revelation. *They reject the idea that man unaided has achieved his own humanistic improvement.* Neither do these religions accept that man did, or could, arrive at the religious concept of monotheism by speculative thinking, however close to that achievement Plato may have arrived. To believers of these three religions, monotheism, as revealed in the Old and New Testaments and in the Qor'an, is the manner by which man may retain his spirituality in an enveloping desert of atheistic materialism.[5] [Emphasis added].

Draper's point is that monotheism or its subset, monotruism, is a choice, a matter of faith. There is no evidence of universal objective truth. It cannot be found unless it is first imagined and collectively revered. While secularization has deep historical roots in monotheism, it is revolutionary for our time because it insists upon abandoning skepticism which has been the bedrock of liberal democracies and specifically, Postmodern Secularism. Postmodern secularism creates conflict because it *assumes* conflict.

Monotheistic faith is no different than the faith of secularists. All great achievements are leaps of faith: the Enlightenment must have been generated by faith in the existence of an objective world waiting to be rationally discovered. All scientific enquiries are based on faith in a coherent set of principles, of an objective reality. Faith is not the same thing as being religious—faith just means choosing a hopeful, not pessimistic, outcome in the face of uncertainty. We cannot reach a unity based on diversity, or bring heaven to earth, unless we first believe in it and make a collective commitment to it. The Judeo-Christian view of secularization—which assigns the responsibility to reconcile the three forms to individuals—has not been explicitly identified as a political objective in the United States. The political crisis will not be resolved until the wall is placed in the larger context of the U-shaped plot. The only other choice is the inverse plot of human tragedy (∩).

SECULARIZATION AND THE LIBERAL TRADITION

> The health of a democratic society may be measured by the quality of functions performed by private citizens
> —Alexis De Tocqueville

Secularization requires that when resolving equally valid disputes between rights to equality and freedom of religion, the courts should make their decisions on the basis of encouraging the collective pursuit of truth. The strongest endorsement for secularization over secularism mirrors Oliver Wendell Holmes' justification for freedom of speech. Holmes' justifications did not support equality or even freedom as absolute values, but rather for the sake of protecting the pursuit and dissemination of truth. Commitment to objective truth is the American political anchor of monotruism over monotheism, of secularization over secularism, of toleration over tolerance.

Secularization supports the wall separating reason from beliefs but sees it as a temporary means of allowing reason the freedom from blasphemy laws that it needs to develop, as well as granting individuals their freedom of experiences, which can then further contribute to science's ability to rationally understand human nature. The process of seeking a universal truth regarding human nature must continue until one theory is universally acknowledged as both objectively, and subjectively, true.

Secularization is rooted in the liberal tradition. Andrew Murphy in his essay "Tolerance, Toleration and the Liberal tradition," similarly revealed significant confusion in the academic literature between the terms tolerance and toleration. Murphy stated that distinguishing between tolerance, being one's *personal* attitude of not judging others, and toleration, as being a *state* policy of remaining neutral, was necessary in order to properly understand the liberal tradition. Murphy argued that traditional liberalism is best understood as merely state toleration, which does not require that individuals be held to the same standard:

> Universal agreement on attitudes or traits of character, however laudable, remains unlikely. What we can aim for, and what Locke and Williams point toward, are standards of behavior that will allow citizens to negotiate their inevitable differences peacefully. This should not be considered "second-best," but we should not underestimate the difficult task that this sort of toleration places upon us. Still, this "toleration" will likely fall far short of the ideals of many promoting "tolerance." Perhaps however, our choice is more complex: either liberalism with intolerance or tolerance without liberalism.[6]

Secular Hope applies the same structural distinction to secularization and secularism as Murphy applied to toleration and tolerance. Secularization, like toleration, identifies the state's objective as ensuring that all individuals are equally and sufficiently free to contribute to the public debate on human nature, universal truth and morality. While Secularism and Tolerance, both require individuals to also be neutral and suspend their moral judgment. Murphy's analysis of liberalism is excellent, but in his skeptical rejection of the likelihood of universal agreement, he eliminates all hope, and must fall back to the limits of Romantic Secularism.

While liberalism is based on skepticism, it is important to understand that it is not based on nihilism or cynicism, which is the belief that there is no common morality or values and therefore we should not even bother trying to find it. Lord Kenneth Clark, in his 1969 television series "Civilisation", said that cynicism is the enemy of civilization. According to *Merriam-Webster's Collegiate Dictionary*, skepticism is "the doctrine that true knowledge or knowledge in a particular area is uncertain; the method of suspended judgment, systematic doubt, or criticism characteristic of skeptics."[7] Suspended judgment is not the same thing as never judging. Richard Niebuhr put it this way: "It is not apparent that one who knows that his concepts are not universal must also doubt that they are concepts of the universal."[8]

Plato, Augustine, Aquinas, Locke, and Hobbes all believed that reason and faith could, and should, be reconciled. In the spirit of secularization, Locke argued that reason was the final arbiter, but revelation must also be included in any reasonable conclusion:

> Reason must be our last judge and guide in everything. I do not mean that we must consult reason, and examine whether a proposition revealed from God can be made out by natural principles, and if it cannot, that then we may

reject it: but consult it we must, and by it examine
whether it be a revelation from God or no: and
if reason finds it to be revealed from God, reason
then declares for it as much as for any other truth,
and makes it one of her dictates. [9]

Further, to love truth, as Locke clearly did, is to endorse
secularization, not secularism. Locke wrote in a letter:

To love truth for truth's sake is the principal part
of human perfection in this world, and the seed-
plot of all other virtues. [10]

Secularization is able to overcome skepticism by extending
the time-horizon of hope. Secularization encourages the reconciliation of all three means of knowing truth, both on the
individual and societal levels. It encourages citizens to collectively
articulate an objective truth regarding human nature that can
accommodate everyone's subjective experiences. Secularization
requires that the state promote such interactions, wherever
possible, therein promoting unity in diversity, promised by the
myth of monotheism.

While reaching universal consensus on human nature seems
like a remote possibility, it merely requires more sophisticated
discussions on the relative strengths and weaknesses of each form
of knowledge. Religion's strength is its longevity, and its inspiring
nature. Reason and science's strength are their universality, demand
for proof and ability to distinguish cause and effect. Personal
experiences are obviously the most relevant to understanding
human nature and can easily identify strong correlations, but are
subject to unconscious conditioning and failing to distinguish
cause and effect (denial and projection). Secularization envisions
absolute truth as the trinity of three forms of knowledge, resolved
over time and cultures. One day, the words of Ptah, the god of
creation, will be understood.

INTERNATIONAL COSTS OF SECULARISM

By failing to distinguish between secularism and secularization, and then by associating secularism with modernity, Western academics have contributed to the dangerous black-and-white thinking that has given rise to Huntington's *The Clash of Civilizations*. Consider how Bernard Lewis has framed progress in a linear fashion, such that Muslims feel they have no choice but to go backward in order to preserve their cultural values: "The rejection of modernity in favor of return to the sacred past has a varied and ramified history in the region."[11]

Lewis' faulty assumption was to reject all religion and myth as illogical, and to declare progress to be the eradication of religion, not reconciliation of religion and reason. Talal Asad expressed the demoralizing nature of secularist assumptions this way: "Western modernity is therefore thought to be pregnant with positive futures in a way that no other cultural condition is".[12] Because we live in a globalized world, how the West defines itself affects how other cultures understand themselves.

By declaring the superiority of secularism, without clearly defining it, the West is inadvertently promoting fundamentalism. Secularism is, unfortunately, the cracked bedrock of most foreign policy decisions, and is used to justify wars in the name of freedom. By becoming aware of our common mythos as monotheistic cultures, we can more responsibly secularize faith and allow our creative energies to find ways to support different paths to post-modernity. This line of thinking is explored further in Chapter Six.

MOST HAVE ALREADY STARTED THE CLIMB

Secularization is a matter of faith, and the good news is that the majority of people in the West already show signs of that faith. Empirical evidence shows that mono*truism* is a widely held belief, while absolute mono*theists* and moral relativists are comparatively rare. This is demonstrated by polls that find, despite significantly declining religious behaviors, belief in God is actually still quite high in secular societies: 92 percent in the United States,[13] and 84 percent in Canada.[14] While European percentages are lower, atheists do not yet make up the majority. This data speaks to the idea that a majority of Westerners, if not all, believe in one universal truth, because the remainder likely believe exclusively in one truth achieved through science. Very few are willing to follow Rorty into a postmodern world of moral relativity. It would be interesting to see polling results on the following questions:

- Do you believe that there is one universal truth regarding human nature?

- Should society try to reconcile legal and religious morality?

- Who should be the final decision maker in that reconciliation process?

Also encouraging is the evidence that a majority of religious believers no longer believe in the second and third exclusive commitments of monotheism. That the religious right is trying to get the creation theory accepted as an alternative scientific theory, as opposed to shutting down schools, shows that they are not exclusive in their commitment to revelation as the only legitimate path to truth.

On the third level, the Pew Forum on Religion and Public Life found that a majority of American believers acknowledged that there is more than one religious path to spiritual truth. A survey conducted in the summer of 2008 found that among Christians who say that many religions can lead to eternal life (65 percent of all Christians); the vast majority (80 percent) cites an example of at least one non-Christian religion that can lead to salvation. Sixty-one percent name two or more non-Christian religions, and even among evangelical Protestants, 72 percent name at least one non-Christian religion that can also lead to salvation. The third exclusive commitment of monotheism, that "my religion is the only right one" has largely disappeared in the West.

Understanding secularization as a U-shaped mythos is to secularize hope, faith, and charity; hope in a peaceful outcome, faith in our common humanity, and the charitable agreement to disagree in the meanwhile. Secularization is simply admitting that scepticism is appropriate for reason, in the face of significant democratic opposition. The following are potential benefits of America formally adopting secularization, as opposed to secularism, as a constitutional principle:

1. Secularization would provide America with a new symbolic path of progress, retaining and celebrating America's unique political history, but providing for a more hopeful future;

2. By identifying the pursuit of truth as the highest political value, this political framework would provide a safe, rational means of bringing the best aspects of religion (hope, meaning, and respect for truth) into the political public sphere and neutrally resolve the current political impasse;

3. This new symbol of U shaped progress would reposition America's unique path to modernity as one that may be joined with alternative paths (see more details in Chapter Six);

4. This broader perspective would facilitate the development of a much-needed global ethics capable of addressing the urgent moral issues of global warming, nuclear weapons and bioethics.

Given that those who drive the political debates are not those already happily sitting on the wall of separation, the following three chapters each make a specialized appeal. Chapter Four is aimed at monotheists who are trying to pull the wall down. It shows how secularization is not just about reconciling religion and politics, but is also for reconciling contradictory messages within religious scripture. In Chapter Five, three different arguments are presented for those who are trying to plug all the holes in the wall of separation. Chapter Six explores the works of Muslim academics and shows how their criticisms of secularism can be accommodated by the secularization thesis, in hope that they can envision their own secularization process.

Chapters Seven and Eight are legal in nature and will be of most interest to those concerned with constitutional law, because they show how seemingly slight differences in the Canadian and American constitutions have taken the two countries in significantly different directions. Finally, Chapter Nine returns to the current American political climate and makes some projections and recommendations about future political alliances and how they could positively influence the American economy and foreign relations.

NOTES

1. Lee and O'Grady (eds.) Collected Works of Northrop Frye, Vol. 4, p.14–15.

2. Ibid, 21.

3. Ibid, 16.

4. Harvey Cox, The Secular City, (NY: Macmillan Company, 1965) 20.

5. The Concept of Monotheism in Islam and Christianity Papers of the International Symposium organized in Rome, Italy, 17–19 November 1981, under the patronage of H. R. H. Crown Prince Hassan of Jordan by the International Progress Organization. http://i-p-o.org/islam-christianity-contents.htm 39.

6. Andrew R. Murphy, "Tolerance, Toleration, and the Liberal Tradition" Polity, Volume 9, 1997.

7. http://www.merriam-webster.com/dictionary/skepticism

8. Richard Niebuhr, The Meaning of Revelation (New York: MacMillian, 1941) 18.

9. John Locke, An Essay Concerning Human Understanding, Book 4, Chapter 19, Para. 14 in An Essay Concerning Human Understanding, John Locke, Volume 2, edited by. A.C. Fraser (Toronto: Dover Publications, 1959) p. 438.

10. Letter to Anthony Collins (29 October 1703) in E. S. De Beer, The Correspondence of John Locke Vol. 8 (Oxford: Clarendon Press, 1989) 97.

11. Bernard Lewis, "The Revolt of Islam—When did the conflict with the West begin, and how could it end?" The New Yorker, November 19, 2001.

12. Saba Mahmood, Standford Electronic Humanities Review, volume 5.1, Issue 1 "Interview with Talal Asad Modern power and the reconfiguration of religious traditions" Updated February 27, 1996. http://www.stanford.edu/group/SHR/5-1/text/toc.html

13. Pew Forum on Religion and Public Life Survey, U.S. Religious Landscape Survey, 2009

14. Online: http://pewforum.org/docs/?DocID=265

15. According to Statistics Canada's 2001 Census, 16.4 percent of Canadians identified themselves as having no religious affiliation. In the US, a significant portion of the religiously affiliated still believed in God, so the Canadian figure is likely higher.

CHAPTER 4 –
APPEAL TO MONOTHEISTS

> The Worst Corruption is a Corrupt Religion
> —Reinhold Niebuhr

The worst corruption is religious corruption, because it turns faith upside down. Corrupt religious leaders will claim the greatest faith when they actually have no faith at all. They have faith in a universal truth that is accurate—but they fear that it does not include them. So they feel the urgent need to project their own subjective truth as God's will. This of course then requires the bullying of others to ensure they act in concert with the "universal truth of God's will". Faithless religious leaders succeed in proving their only true belief: which is that it is indeed evil to have no faith. The genuinely faithful must reclaim universal truth from the faithless.

The worst corruption is religious corruption because it turns truth upside down. This happens when our ability to reason is not mature enough to understand how our incredibly different "natures" could possibly be created and loved by one God. We fear that one of us must not belong. In order to quiet that fear, we insist that our "nature" is universal and consider only the evidence that supports our truth. God's objective truth can withstand the scrutiny of reason and the granting human rights and freedoms, subjective truth cannot.

Romantic Secularism protected religion against internal corruption in many ways. It ensured universal education and the granting of civil rights. It allowed everyone the political freedom to withdraw their support from religious leaders who have lost their faith. Finally, secular societies created independent legal systems to which religious leaders could be held accountable for their criminal and fraudulent acts. Romantic Secularism has allowed American faith to mature and thrive by empowering individuals to test and validate their religious truths against their personal experiences and reason.

MONOTHEISM AND THE HOLY SCRIPTURES

When traditional monotheism is understood as logos, or taken literally, it can create many internal contradictions. The anthropomorphic, but abstract Yahweh, the Christian Trinity, and the Islamic tradition of affirming Judaism and Christianity with AHAD, the one God, are all very difficult concepts to reconcile logically, until God is understood as a metaphor for the one truth regarding human nature. Absolute monotheists are not true believers because they must contradict large portions of their own scriptures to justify their tyranny. Irony and hypocrisy will always expose the faithless.

The following excerpts from the 1981 interfaith meeting on "The concept of monotheism in Islam and Christianity" support this narrower interpretation of monotruism, over monotheism. G.I.A.D. Draper in his written contribution, "The Historical Background of the Concept of Monotheism," describes the first anthropomorphic monotheistic God Yahweh:

> Apart from being Creator of All, the Israelite YAHWEH is alone, without consort or son or

daughter ... Deep in the Israelite consciousness
of YAHWEH is His anthropomorphic nature ...
The attributes of YAHWEH are those possessed
also by human beings, such as rage, envy, hatred,
revenge and sorrow, but these are possessed by
Him in epic measure.[15]

Draper continues the story of monotheism as it leads into
Christianity:

The anthropomorphic idea of God of the early
Israelite phase returns full circle with the human
qualities of YAHWEH spiritualized. Now, for the
first time, the ever-present menace of polytheism
has abated and Christianity can, as it were, afford
the expansion of the idea of one God with three
hypostases, complementary in functions but
leaving monotheism intact. In the first, he is now
closer to man than the Israelite YAHWEH. In
the second, he is the sole Creator and Ruler of the
Universe as He was to the Deutero-Isaiah. In the
third, he is the Holy Spirit or Paraclete or Divine
Wisdom. This threefold hypostasis has enriched
monotheism and has, in the view of Christian
scholars, not detracted from it.

At the interfaith meeting, an Islamic explanation of
monotheism was delivered by Nassir El-Din El-Assad, President
of the Royal Academy for Islamic Civilization Research (as it
was then named) in the Inaugural Lecture on Behalf of H.R.H.
Crown Prince Hassan of Jordan. Note the contradiction between
the clear statement that there is only one God and the equally clear
message that the Qur'ân affirms Judaism and Christianity, making
a strong argument against monotheism, and for monotruism.
[El-Assad's numbering is included to assist in referencing the
original text].

3. In the Holy Qor'an two words are used to describe the Oneness of God. The first word is "AHAD" and the second is WAHID. The first word AHAD is used as an adjective. Say "He is the one God." It has been used in two Surahs to deny that God has any partner or companion associated with Him. This form of the word "AHAD" indicates that God is unique, that He is One and has always been One and has never had any other one with Him. In Arabic, linguistically, this form means "the negation of any other number."

When reading the following passages on WAHID, consider how beautifully they read when "God" is substituted for "truth" and put into a political context:

The second word "WAHID" may mean the same as the first word and is used many times in the Qor'an to indicate this meaning. However, it also has another meaning and that is "the One, Same God for all." This is revealed in the address by God to the People of the Book (the Scriptures). When He says to them, "Your God is One" or when He says, "We believe in that which has been revealed to us and revealed to you, and that our God and your God is one and the same, to whom we submit".

Consequently, there is only one God for Moslems, and He is the same God for all peoples. This means the unity of God and the unity of his message.

The unity of God and His message is mentioned frequently in the Holy Qor'an, and God demands that we believe that since Noah, Abraham, Jacob, Moses, and Jesus are all messengers, prophets of God, we should not differentiate between them, and that the books revealed to them are His books, and every one of these books affirms the belief in what has come before it. In fact, the Qor'an is an affirmation of what has preceded it. The prophet Mohammed said, "The prophets are brothers, their mothers are different, but their religion is one, and the same."

4. On TAWHID—Creatures should not direct their prayers, hopes, fears, or desires to anyone except God. They should not ask forgiveness, recovery from illness, success in work, or make any other request to anyone but God. The relationship between God and man is direct; there can be no mediator through whom God speaks to His creatures and through whom favors are requested and sins forgiven.

The best note to end this introduction with is what God asked of Moslems by saying: And do not argue with the People of the Book except in the most kindly way, excluding those who do injustice among them, and say to them: "We believe in that which has been revealed to us and revealed to you, and that our God and your God is one and the same, to whom we submit."[16]

SECULARIZATION AND HUMAN RIGHTS

To secularize monotheism is to consciously declare that we are collectively seeking one truth and are thereby attempting to transcend, not repeat, our violent monotheistic history.

Secularization is the belief that humans will not live divided forever; the metaphoric wall is a *means* of achieving one truth, not the ultimate objective. This means that when the freedoms of speech, religion, conscience, and individual rights in liberal democracies are protected, it is for the collective goal of continually testing and reconciling the three different ways of knowing truth. Dogmatic thinking comes from failing to understand that secularization is a process, and not the final judgment. It is our common humanity that is sacred, not secularism. Our common humanity is the essential core of monotheism, monotruism, secularism, and secularization.

The monotheistic prohibition against false idols can be translated into the idea that all principles must serve the protection and pursuit of truth. There is no higher principle than objective truth; not freedom, diversity, or achieving social or economic equality. But no human being, or political institution, is a god and hence able to declare it unilaterally. Freedom, diversity, and equality are the rewards for reaching truth, not the immediate goals. Equality and freedom are important in that they protect every individual's right to his or her own experiences, which then may be contributed to the global understanding of human nature which serves as the basis of a universal morality. However, equality rights only guarantee state toleration and protection; they do not guarantee universal agreement with each person's definition of the objective truth. Seeking universal truth must rank higher than human rights because it serves our greatest human need—the need to belong.

MONOTRUISTIC COMPROMISE

It is the final proof of God's omnipotence that he need not exist in order to save us
—Peter de Vries

In explaining the resurgence of religion, many academics have pointed out that religion is changing. Many spiritual followers have been characterized as being à la carte believers, rejecting the more doctrinal aspects but retaining the aspects that speak of love and compassion. Militant leaders seeking political power do just the opposite by enforcing the doctrinal elements so strictly that they contradict the religious calls for compassion, respect, and tolerance.

To integrate these two extremes, religious leaders need to reclaim secularization as a religious process. In order to save religion from secularism, religious leaders need to take responsibility for the fact that monotheistic doctrines can be politically dangerous and promote violence; while spiritual leaders need to acknowledge the dangers of moral relativism. Monotheism's second and third levels of exclusive commitment need to be clearly rejected as signs of lack of faith. The gain for such a compromise is that secularization confirms there is one truth and there is a role for religion in ascertaining that one truth. Further, individuals in non-government capacities can publicly express their religious morality in a civil manner and can vote on the basis of those values.

However, it should be remembered that reconciliation is a two-way street. Alan Wolfe and John Rawls are correct in requiring that sovereign legitimacy must have a rational foundation, as it is the only universal language. Incorporation of religious beliefs into policy via popular vote is at best a temporary solution. The only responsible way to resolve the debate is to deconstruct religious myths in order to reveal their wisdom. The real test of faith will be those who seek to rationally explain their religious beliefs. Northrop Frye encouraged this:

> The church has been tempted by the world to present its faith as an obstinate reiteration of its traditional myths, insisting on the teeth of all natural law that they are facts, and defying the

> advance of science as a dog howls at the rising moon. It must learn to present its faith as the emancipation and fulfillment of reason. It has been tempted by the world to condemn human liberty as an illicit encroachment on the divine prerogative. It must learn to explain once more how it is God's will that man should be free.[17]

Political history has been a fight between church and state over the right of individuals to have their own experiences. In liberal societies, that freedom puts a serious strain on the unity of the society, but those experiences also present valuable opportunities to uncover the unrevealed wisdom in religions. Believers need to focus on the long-term task. Currently, advertising executives have a better understanding of human nature, and this expertise needs to be reclaimed by religious leaders. While believers must prove the rationality of their moral beliefs, secularism has granted them an array of learning opportunities to empirically demonstrate consequences that would not be permitted in nonsecular societies. Rationally proving one's faith is only possible in a secularizing society. If the religious community fails to do so, their only option will be to continue running expensive political campaigns.

Because America has such distinct communities with strong biases in their preferred form of knowledge such as Hollywood (sentiment and sensation), Utah (religion), and academia (reason), America will likely be at the forefront of such reconciliation efforts. America's diverse communities will become its strength, once given the secularization framework within which they can work out their differences. America will one day be known for balancing its respect for individual differences with its faith in the rationality of their religious beliefs.

NOTES

1. The Concept of Monotheism in Islam and Christianity Papers of the International Symposium organized in Rome, Italy, 17–19 November 1981, under the patronage of H. R. H. Crown Prince Hassan of Jordan by the International Progress Organization. http://i-p-o.org/islam-christianity-contents. htm p.36.

2. Ibid, 23–5.

3. Lee and O'Grady, (eds.) Collected Works of Northrop Frye, vol. 4, 267.

CHAPTER 5 –
APPEAL TO SECULARISTS

> Liberty cannot be established without morality, nor morality
> without Faith
> — Alexis De Tocqueville

Secularists must break with their faith in reason long enough to realize "It is only the language of the imagination that can take us beyond the imagination."[1] In this quotation, Frye is saying that only by understanding the language of myth can we get beyond our religious past. This is why the metaphoric wall of separation keeps bringing us back to religion, not past it. To most secularists, the wall protects their individual experiences against the judgment of religion. However, secularists should not confuse their objective with their means; otherwise, they risk losing the protection of the wall altogether.

Three arguments are presented in this chapter to convince secularists of the importance of the idea of there being one truth, thus converting them from Postmodern Secularism to secularization. The first is a secular interpretation of the biblical prohibition against false idols. The second argument demonstrates how liberals make the argument for Postmodern Secularism (live and let live) but consistently reveal their monotruistic beliefs. In conclusion, some of the views of Jürgen Habermas, a leading humanist philosopher, are presented as the final argument supporting secularization over secularism.

IN DEFENSE OF ELIMINATING FALSE GODS

This section explores another aspect of monotheism; its prohibition against false idols. The following two quotations from Northrop Frye provide a good introduction:

> We can hardly overestimate the importance, for our own cultural tradition, of the fact that Biblical monotheism, the basis of Judaism, Christianity, and Islam, is a revolutionary movement, totally different in social context and reference from imperial monotheism.[2]

> The revolutionary monotheism of the Bible develops a hatred of "idolatry," and an idol is essentially a visual image of something authoritative or numinous in nature: all the divinities that have been discovered in nature are devils, and the chosen people listen to the voice of its invisible God. [3]

These may appear to be a poor start for convincing secularists of the humanist value of monotheism, but consider this interpretation: monotheism was radical for its time, and continues to be today, because it asserts an ideal human nature that cannot be *seen* in nature. For instance, money may buy attractive clothes and cars, easily diverting one's attention from the invisible ideal of human generosity. If humans do not actively remind themselves of the invisible ideal, they will believe that looking good is superior to being good, and an idol (false God or false truth) of physical beauty is created, and necessarily human generosity will suffer. Because beauty is *naturally* compelling, if our personal experiences and reasoning become our only inputs for determining truth, beauty becomes our highest truth, and therefore our highest human potential.

Consider for a moment that children today are being breastfed with silicone breasts; and young boys are emulating grown men who have spray-tanned muscles created solely to win trophies for striking poses. Ironically, when we worship human nature, we become unnatural because we strip beauty of its virtue. That is because beauty alone, like all false idols, does not lead to happiness. With unwavering faith however, humans will worship false gods until they become exaggerated, addicting, and ultimately ugly. Irony proves God's sense of humor.

A rebuttal in the spirit of Rousseau is that it is also in our nature to be good, generous, and kind. This is true, but it is very difficult to create a visual idol of these qualities, and because it is also human nature to be most influenced by what we see, we must continually discipline ourselves against false idols. An honest critique of Western society, with its increasing gap between the rich and the poor, corporate fraud, rampant child pornography, increased human trafficking and slavery, strongly suggests that we need to find a more effective way to publicly support these naturally good attributes which consistently get second-billing to materialism.

The limits of Romanticism become apparent when human nature is not just freed, but worshipped. The result is narcissism where individuals lacking in shame, can no longer differentiate between self-esteem and selfishness, fame and respect, legitimate business and fraud. Harvey Cox phrased it in a way that is most appropriate in this age of climate change:

> The mature secular man neither reverences nor ravages nature. His task is to tend it and make use of it, to assume the responsibility assigned to The Man, Adam. [4]

When we dismiss the warning against false idols, merely because it is written in mythical language, we risk losing our greatest inheritance: common belief in our unrealized potential for good. There is significant current value in understanding monotheism. Pure rationality without imagination, can only lead us back to our past, like the Greek concept of time that goes around in endless circles. Postmodern Secularism offers diversity as another false god. Because it is grounded in the absolute worst example of human nature, it will not be able to take us beyond our past.

PICKING AND CHOOSING

Liberal theorists, or advocates, consistently show a pattern of both defending their own freedoms and majority votes, but then deny others both their liberty and democratic votes, in the name of tolerance. They can accomplish this by switching between different forms of secularism. They use Romantic Secularism to advance their freedoms, but then seek protection behind the diversity argument when others seek the freedom to advance their concept of human nature. This is not done vindictively. It is based on legitimate evidence but of a limited sample, on the faulty assumption that reason is always superior to religion; and because it is very hard to give up one's belief in right and wrong.

By failing to clearly define the philosophic assumptions of secularism, liberals may jump back and forth, and appear rational and righteous while they prevent others from exercising their freedom of conscience. For example, John Rawls argued that freedom of conscience could not be fully realized unless individuals belonging to a minority could see themselves as worthy of respect; therefore the state had a role to play in ensuring this outcome:

> Self-respect is rooted in our self-confidence as a fully cooperating member of society capable of pursuing a worthwhile conception of the good over the complete life.[5]

While this is a worthy objective and is consistent with the postmodern objective of *ensuring* diversity, implementing it politically requires putting limits on other citizens' freedom of conscience and/or speech, and thereby violating Romantic Secularism's commitment to neutrality on non-material issues and beliefs. It is essentially unfair because the structure of equality rights does not extend the same protection of self-respect to those who belong to the majority. By not distinguishing between Romantic Secularism and Postmodern Secularism, liberals are able to take advantage of the protection afforded by the wall of separation, while denying its protection to others who disagree with their view of human nature.

As a second example, Alan Wolfe, in his book *The Future of Liberalism*, acknowledged that while the "liberal temperament" is not a core principle of liberalism, it is a common characteristic of liberals to fight for the underdog:

> The liberal temperament has more to do with psychology than with politics or morality. "Liberalism" in this meaning of the term seeks to include rather than exclude, to accept rather than censor, to respect rather than to stigmatize, to welcome rather than reject, to be generous and appreciative rather than stingy and mean. [6]

Wolfe then describes how this personality characteristic evolves into reform initiatives aimed at dissolving the private/public distinction in a monotruistic fashion and is justified by using the very unhelpful term 'evil':

To be sure, liberals recognize that evil can lurk in the hearts of men and women and that some political systems—by definition, illiberal ones—have been evil in the extreme. But they hold that the existence of the bad does not make impossible the realization of the good. On the contrary, the fact that some societies lack liberalism's generosity of spirit is all the more reason for liberals *to insist on reform, not only in the public and political sense but in the private and human one.* [Emphasis added].

Wolfe, like almost everyone from a monotheistic culture, desires that there be one common morality, with no divide between public and private beliefs, and that their ideal view of human nature become the ideal. Wolfe's yearning is the remnant of monotheism that has never really been abandoned.

By keeping the political debate framed as one of reason versus religion, secularists don't have to admit to their own monotruistic desires for right and wrong, and their own potential for slipping into Rational Secularism on specific issues. Because Wolfe believes that tolerance is neutral, he genuinely sees no condescension in his desire to "reform" both public and private beliefs. Tolerance is a neutral value theoretically, but in the same way that feminists pointed out in the 1980's, with reference to equality, enforced neutrality merely entrenches any existing prejudices or power imbalances.

Not all power imbalances are readily articulated, but that does not mean they do not exist. When feminists rightfully demanded equality they focused on male forms of power (physical, financial, political). However, uniquely female forms of power were not included in that discussion.[7] In many areas, but especially on gender dynamics and sexuality, science and reason have not sufficiently evolved to justify politically cutting off other forms of knowledge (experience and religion). To confidently declare an end to the gender wars and to say that the time for neutral tolerance has arrived, despite significant opposition, is to seriously contradict the values of freedom of conscience and democracy. It requires a level of cynicism and dogma that is found in Rational Secularism.

Finally, liberal commitment to monotruism is also demonstrated by the GLBT (Gay, Lesbian, Bisexual, and Transgender) community when it expresses dissatisfaction with the private/public divide. For example, when the GLBT community in New Orleans purposely holds its annual Gay parade on the Easter weekend, it is not celebrating the diversity of beliefs; it is making a political statement about right and wrong. As another example, consider the following article by Bert Archer, a syndicated columnist from Toronto who wrote about gay marriage in June 2009:

> We changed a lot of laws to let these people marry each other, and upset a lot of people in the process—all for what's turned out to be something like 0.06 per cent of the population. Was it all worth it? The short answer is no. The government's only callable interest in its constituents marrying is the production of more citizens, more taxpayers and while same-sex coupling doesn't do any harm to that formula, it doesn't help it either.
>
> The long answer, however, is yes. What the government did when it changed all those laws was create a different Canada. It had been a long time since we led the world, Medicare was great, and we were once Pearson's peacekeepers. But other than Celine Dion and the Blackberry, what had we done for the world lately? Six years ago this month, we became only the third nation in

the world to let same-sex couples marry. From
that point on, the rest of the world has been
playing catch up.[8]

The point is not whether gay marriage is morally right or
wrong; the point is that Archer admits the policy goes beyond the
state's material or secular interest, contradicting the very secular
premise of government neutrality that granted homosexuals
their human rights in the first place. Pierre Trudeau summarized
it beautifully when he was Minister of Justice: "The state has
no business in the bedrooms of the nation."[9] The Postmodern
equivalent is "The state has no business dictating the spiritual
beliefs of the nation". But Archer sees no contradiction because he
has seamlessly changed his version of secularism from government
neutrality to promoting tolerance.

While on the topic of same-sex marriage, it is now worth
discussing its similarities and differences with the issue of
forced racial segregation in the American south. It is true that
both involve an active judiciary and equality rights. However,
protecting the spiritual aspect of marriage from judicial review
is not fully comparable because on the issue of segregation, the
judiciary was acting in concert with the democratic support of a
federal majority. The court was forcing social change on a powerful
minority that was using terrorist tactics. Further, the judiciary was
squarely within its jurisdictional boundaries because the offenders
were enjoying *material gain* from their discriminatory *actions and
laws* that caused significant *material and economic harm* to other
citizens.

Religious believers today are asking the judiciary to preserve
the spiritual aspect of marriage per Romantic Secularism's promise
to respect the divide between spiritual and material issues. Further
they are not seeking to maintain an unjust economic advantage.[10]
As of October, 2009, 57% of all Americans supported civil unions
for same-sex couples, while only 39 percent supported same-
sex marriage. Since Obama announced the extension of equal

benefits under civil unions, an increasing number of opponents to same-sex marriage are now endorsing civil unions, up from 24% to 30%.[11] Further evidence of the non-economic foundation of the conflict is demonstrated by the fact that many Republicans are sacrificing economic gain by rejecting government spending programs, like healthcare reform, as a means of maintaining a small government, which they vehemently equate with protecting their religious beliefs. This issue is about protecting the spiritual aspect of marriage.

President Obama has reached a thoughtful compromise by allowing civil unions to receive all the material benefits of marriage. That the GLBT community is not satisfied with this compromise proves that there is more at play than civil rights. There is a spiritual aspect to marriage for which they are seeking equal recognition. This is an understandable, legitimate request but is not the state's to provide. Obama's solution respects the secular limitations of the state, but this solution needs to be permanently anchored in the rationality of secularization by appealing to the higher goal of seeking a universal, objective truth.

Neither the religious right nor the GLBT can prove the implications of same-sex marriage because there is not enough time to properly evaluate its impact. To argue that conclusive proof that children of same-sex marriages have not been impacted, when a full generation has not yet matured cannot be good science. Until sufficient time has passed to make these assessments properly, the issue should be decided democratically, at the state level. Individual state differences are the perfect result for gathering more evidence. The best that can be done at this point is to put faith in the Constitution, and let each community live and work out their differences in real-life contexts. One day, one side or the other will be able to provide proof of their assertions. The truth will come out if the state does not short-circuit that process and declare a winner prematurely.

Liberal democrats should consider the underlying assumptions of their arguments and whether or not they are changing those assumptions depending on which side of the argument they find themselves. If they are postmodern advocates for moral relativity, they must conclude that everyone's beliefs need to be respected as equally untouchable. Alternatively, they could declare they believe in one moral truth with no public/private divide. If so, however, they would then need to determine whether they are committed to the democratic secularization process, or if they are Rational Secularists and believe in the suppression of religion, and the personal experiences of believers.

What they cannot do is claim to be defenders of freedom, while denying others their freedom of conscience. Of course, they could do so, but in that case they should reconsider calling themselves liberal democrats. Being clearer about one's assumptions and principles will significantly improve the quality of the political debates, and help everyone to identify the occasions when they are not holding themselves to the same standards they are holding others. The following flowchart in Diagram 5-1 shows how to classify these differing political assumptions and beliefs.

As noted previously, Peter Berger stated that the human need for certainty is a primary cause for the religious resurgence:

> Clearly, one of the most important topics for a sociology of contemporary religion is precisely this interplay of secularizing and counter-secularizing forces. This is because modernity, for fully understandable reasons, undermines all the old certainties; uncertainty, in turn is a condition that many people find very hard to bear; therefore, any movement (not only a religious one) that promises to provide or to renew certainty has a ready market.[12]

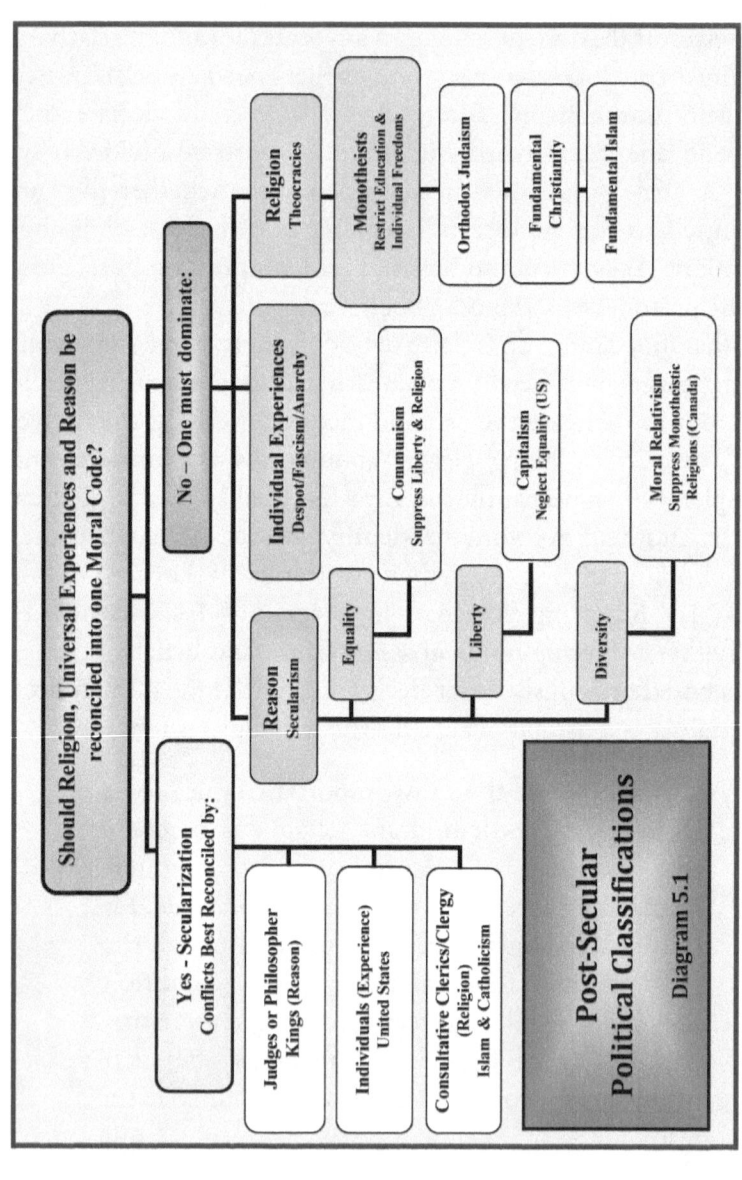

Postsecular Political Classifications

Should Religion, Universal Experiences and Reason be reconciled into one Moral Code?

Yes – Secularization
Conflicts Best Reconciled by:

Judges or Philosopher Kings (Reason)

Individuals (Experience) United States

Consultative Clerics/Clergy (Religion) Islam & Catholicism

No – One must dominate:

Reason
Secularism

Individual Experiences
Despot/Fascism/Anarchy

Religion
Theocracies

Monotheists
Restrict Education & Individual Freedoms

Orthodox Judaism

Fundamental Christianity

Fundamental Islam

Equality

Liberty

Diversity

Communism
Suppress Liberty & Religion

Capitalism
Neglect Equality (US)

Moral Relativism
Suppress Monotheistic Religions (Canada)

Post-Secular Political Classifications

Diagram 5.1

If certainty is the need to believe in one truth, it has been shown that both secularists and believers have this need, and will tend to impose their versions of "truth" on others if they are not politically prevented from doing so. It is this monotruistic drive to be understood and respected that still needs to be tempered by the wall of separation until a universal understanding of human nature is reached.

Today's political conflicts reflect the profound changes of moving from the rigid personal identities automatically provided by the mythos of patriarchy, to a more flexible, rationally expressed vision of human nature and gender. That process is not yet complete and therefore the wall of separation needs to remain. The next section of this Chapter takes a different approach in explaining why government neutrality is so important.

HABERMAS ON RELIGION AND RATIONALITY

> Truth springs from arguments amongst friends.
> —David Hume

As the final argument for convincing secularists of the value in secularization, some of the views of Jürgen Habermas, a leading humanist philosopher, are presented. Habermas locates both rationality, and the greatest potential for conflict, in language. In response to this problem, Habermas developed his theory of communicative action, which is consistent with the objectives of secularization.

Habermas clearly cannot be given justice here, but an extremely brief summary is that moral certainty can only be achieved when individuals speak directly to each other about their ethical differences. Personal dialogue allows for other means of communication to transcend the limitations of language. Further, exacerbating the limitations of language, when we discuss ethical differences through political or religious organizations, we lose sight of our adversaries' humanity. Not surprisingly then, we too readily fail to find common ground, and we justify our own coercion or violence.

In addition to personal dialogue, Habermas promotes the ongoing process of reconciling religious and rational truths because he believes that religion still holds value that is inaccessible to reason:

> The process of a critical appropriation of the essential contents of religious tradition is still underway and the outcome is difficult to predict. I willingly repeat my position: "As long as religious language bears with itself inspiring, indeed, unrelinquishable semantic contents which elude (for the moment?) the expressive power of a philosophical language and still await translation into a discourse that gives reasons for its positions, philosophy, even in its postmetaphysical form, will neither be able to replace nor repress religion.[14]

Habermas also supports the idea that monotheist traditions can still have much to contribute to secular understanding and renewal of Western culture:

> Today the ecclesial communities are in competition with other communities of interpretation that are rooted in secular traditions. Even viewed from outside, it could turn out that monotheist traditions have at their disposal a language whose semantic potential is not yet exhausted, [unabgegoltenen], that shows itself superior in its power to disclose the world and to form identity, in its capability for renewal, its differentiation, and its range.[15]

Indirectly supporting the secularization thesis, Habermas explains God metaphorically:

> God is the name for that substance that gives coherence, unity, and thickness to the life-world wherein humans dwell seeking to acknowledge each other as meaning-giving creatures.[16]

> "God" becomes the name for a communicative structure that forces men, on the pain of a loss of their humanity, to go beyond their accidental, empirical nature to encounter one another indirectly, that is, across an objective something that they themselves are not.[17]

Habermas defines God as a concept that requires humans to give meaning to each other's existence—or as the common pursuit of truth through a political process that allows everyone to have their experiences heard and understood. This ideal most closely resembles secularization, which assigns the task of reconciling reason and revelation to individuals (as opposed to a judiciary, theologians, or Plato's philosopher kings). Habermas' definition of God also explains why so many people living in secular countries continue to say they believe in God but do not go to church or identify themselves with a particular religion.

Just as Jefferson and his rational skeptics of the Enlightenment ironically became political bedmates with the extremely religious Puritans and Anabaptists in erecting the wall separating church and state, Jürgen Habermas, as a humanist philosopher, has more in common with the religious right than with secular atheists. Habermas and the religious right share the hope and faith of reconciling reason and religion through individual dialogue, not through institutional rules limited to existing theories of human nature.

While it is critical to understand history and guard against potentially dangerous totalitarianism, it is also important to look ahead. Reason and faith can be reconciled if there is faith in both reason and religion. Secularization can accommodate both the hope offered by religion, and the inclusiveness promised by secularists.

NOTES

1. Lee and O'Grady, Frye's Collected Works, 22.

2. Imperial monotheism is forcing conquered people to take on the religion of the new king or a king's new religion.

3. Lee and O'Grady, Frye's Collected Works, 11-12.

4. Cox, The Secular City, 23.

5. John Rawls, Political Liberalism, (New York: Columbia University Press, 1993) 318.

6. Alan Wolfe, The Future of Liberalism, (New York: Alfred A Knopf, 2009) 19.

7. The HBO series "The Sopranos" brilliantly explores the female forms of power in the patriarchal context of an Italian mafia don, providing a post-feminist follow up on the Godfather series.

8. Metro Toronto "Views" June 21, 2009.

9. Former Prime Minister Pierre Trudeau provided this rationale when he was Minister of Justice in December 1967 when proposing a bill to decriminalize acts of sodomy which came into force in 1969.

10. Pew Research Centre Publications, http://pewresearch.org/pubs/1375/gay-marriage-civil-unions-opinion.

11. Ibid.

12. Berger, Peter, (ed.) The Desecularization of the World: Resurgent Religion and World Politics, (Grand Rapids MI: William B. Eardman, 1998).

13. The first commitment of monotheism, monotruism which is that there is one unifying truth is not necessarily contradictory to the tenants of pantheism or even polytheism.

14. Jurgen Habermas, Religion and Rationality, Essays on Reason, God and Modernity (Cambridge MA: MIT Polity Press, 2002) 79.

15. Ibid, 70–71.

16. Ibid, 18.

17. Ibid.

CHAPTER 6 –
ISLAMIC SECULARIZATION

This chapter considers whether secularization, as distinct from secularism, might be embraced by Muslims. In an attempt to capture diverse Islamic perspectives, quotations from Sheikh Salman, a Saudi Arabian cleric; Islamic scholar Asghar Ali Engineer from India, as well as John Esposito and Azzam Tamini's book *Islam and Secularism in the Middle East* are each presented and discussed.

Muslims, like many others, are confused about the range of secular societies and the origins of secularism. Particularly confusing to Muslims is why Christianity would support such a concept. Azzam Tamini does his best to explain:

> In the English-language literature on secularism and secularization, political theorists and historians at least agree on one fundamental observation, namely that "secularism" is a product of Christian society ... whether secularization's eventual objective is to deny God and eliminate religion altogether or just to restrict religion to the private sphere while recognizing the existence of a "god" that has no say in people's worldly, or secular, affairs, the concept cannot be

comprehended outside the context of Europe's evolution and its Christian reform movements. Long before the Renaissance, the term "secular" was used to describe functions that were extra-ecclesiastical. The religions establishment itself sanctioned and requested these functions either because priests could not or did not perform them, or in response to changes in social and political circumstances.[1]

The Islamic perception that the Christian churches sanctioned "secularism" rests in the West's own failure to maintain the distinction between secularization and secularism. This oversight is regrettable because there is much to suggest that both fundamental/evangelical Christianity and Islam are quite amenable to secularization.

ISLAMIC VIEWS ON SECULARISM

The following quotations were posted by Sheikh Salman on the popular Islamic Web site "Islam Today".[2] They explain why Islam and secularism are deemed to be incompatible. While strongly worded, they are encouraging to the thesis of *Secular Hope* because they are clearly focused on defending monotheism:

> The conflict between Islam and secularism is none other than the conflict between Islam and polytheism. The differences between Islam and secularism are substantial. The issue at hand is none other than the difference between monotheism and polytheism.

> This Jâhiliyyah of today is exactly like the Jâhiliyyah of old. They say that the mosque is for Allah and everything else is for "Caesar." The schools are for Caesar. The media is for other than

Allah. They restrict Islam to the mosque and the prayer room. Everything else is to be governed without resort to Islamic Law. This is outright polytheism.[3]

It would be interesting to determine if Muslims hold a similar view to Americans regarding the three exclusive claims of absolute monotheism discussed in Chapter Two. In other words, is the Islamic resurgence about belief in the one moral truth, the superiority of revelation over reason, or the superiority of Islam over other religions? In the absence of specific answers, the following opinions address the subject generally. According to Salman's assessment of the compatibility of reason and Islam, the second exclusive commitment to revelation over reason was never supported:

> Islam never experienced the abuses of a Church that took from the people great sums of money, restricted their intellectual lives, and burned their scientists and thinkers, all in the name of religion. Quite the contrary, Muslim history is one of amicability between science and the religion whose first revelation was "Read in the name of your Lord who created." Science is one of the fruits of proper adherence to Islam. It is a result of obeying Allah's command to learn, teach, read, and study.[4]

This next quotation represents a commitment to rationally reject secularism and understand Islam in its historic context:

> We must confront secularism and resist it with every means at our disposal. Two of the most important of these means are as follows:
>
> We must expose and clarify what the secularists are doing. Allah exposed the machinations of the

hypocrites and discusses them in many chapters of the Qur'ân.... *It must be conducted in an objective, factual manner so that even your opponent has no choice but to concede to the truth of what you say.* [Emphasis added]

We must work hard for our religion.... An Arabic verse reads: *"Whoever holds history in his heart has added the lives of others to his own."* We should benefit from the experience of others and realize what the secularists are doing to take over and ruin our societies and make us no more than a small part of the West that reared them. [Emphasis added]

The following quotations from Asghar Ali Engineer are provided to illustrate that there is much in the Qur'ân to lead to rejection of the third assumption of Absolute Monotheism—that Islam is the only path to truth.

Islam can hardly clash with this liberal secularism. The Qur'ân, in fact, directly encourages pluralism vide its verse 5:48. This verse clearly states that every people have their own law and a way i.e. every nation is unique in its way of life, its rules etc. It also says that if Allah had pleased He would have created all human beings a single people but He did not do so in order to test them (whether they can live in harmony with each other despite their differences in laws and way of life). Thus it is clear assertion of pluralism. One must respect the others faith and live in harmony with him/ her.

The Qur'ân also asserts that every people have their own way of worshiping God (see 2:148).

One should not quarrel about this. Instead one should try to excel each other in good deeds. In the verses 60:7–8 we find that Allah will bring about friendship between Muslims and those whom you hold as enemies. And Allah does not forbid you from respecting those who fight you not for religion, nor drive you forth from your homes and deal with them justly. Allah loves doers of justice.

Islam, in fact, is the first religion which legally recognized other religions and gave them dignified status and also accepted the concept of dignity of all children of Adam (17:70) irrespective of their faith, race, tribe, nationality or language (49:13).[5]

Because both Muslim authors reject the second and third exclusive commitments in monotheism, but are still vehemently monotheistic, it must be the first assumption, that of one moral truth, that is attractive. It must be moral relativity that they so strongly oppose. Supporting this conclusion is that the rise in Islamic fundamentalism corresponds with the rise of Postmodern Secularism in the 1980's.

Absolute Monotheism creates problems not just for Postmodern Secularism, but for believers themselves. Islam, Judaism, and Christianity must grapple with the same problem because all three religions have contradictory imperatives for monotheism and tolerance. The challenge is exactly the same. But not all people see it this way. The West wants to believe that it has the advantage in being more tolerant and supportive of individual rights. For example Northrop Frye pointed out the divergence of the two civilizations when he identified the necessity of individual freedom in Judeo-Christian history:

> All societies, including the City of God, are
> free only to the extent that they arrange the
> conditions of freedom for the individual, because
> the individual alone can experience freedom.[6]

Frye argues that individual freedom is the only path to truth and human salvation. A more accurate statement is that individual political freedom is the only way for a Judeo-Christian society to arrive at truth, while remaining faithful to both its religion and reason. Frye's quotation can be equally applied to Islam when the freedom referenced is freedom from ourselves, as opposed to freedom from political authority. Is an Alcoholic free? Are children of divorced parents free from fears of abandonment? Freedom is more than a political right. This is an example of a cultural assumption that shuts down meaningful cross-cultural dialogue that Talal Asad warned against.[7] On a global level, we are all pursuing the same universal truth, therefore only one culture needs to take a fully individualized path to truth, because reason is a universal language; we can learn from each other without having to experience everything firsthand as the next section also argues but this time in the form of a parable.

REUNITING THE PRODIGAL AND OBEDIENT SONS

The shared nature of Western and Islamic challenges can be explored through the parable of the prodigal son. Andrew Murphy, in his book *The Prodigal Nation*, demonstrated how deeply the parable is ingrained in American culture. While the typical articulation of the myth is that America is descending into a moral abyss and therefore needs to return to its strict religious heritage, on a cultural level it is better understood as America deviating from its monotheistic roots. Culturally, the United States has fragmented into many different religions, with different secular concepts of the ideal society. Like the prodigal son who needed to test the validity of his faith through experience, the Western fall is a fall from monotheism. America's return will be a return to monotruism—the full reconciliation of the diversity of human experiences as protected by human rights, reason, and religion.

In comparison, Islam can be understood to be the older brother who obeyed his father, helping to maintain the home to which the prodigal son could return. The parable would be quite different without the older son. The obedient son's concept of morality was broadened by his father's demand for a celebration after his younger brother's return. The father wanted to celebrate because he saw his son's return as a rational and empirical validation of his religion's truth, in addition to the reunification of his family. The older son did not have to make his own journey to learn from his younger brother's choices, or vice versa—the point is "unity through diversity". But the prodigal son (America) does need to come home. Islam preserved the value in monotheism, while America permitted maximum political freedom, allowing for a diversity of human experiences to be rationally studied. America advanced the human ability to rationally understand the natural diversity of human experiences.

The parable of the prodigal son is particularly appropriate when comparing Islam and America because, just like brothers, their animosity is created by their shared values as demonstrated by their mutual desire to please their father, but differing strategies. Muslims do not have to accept the American version of secularization, which assigns the task of reconciling reason and faith to individuals. They can have their own version of post-modernity, their own version of secularization. The U-shaped plot of secularization is wonderfully flexible because non-secular cultures can integrate reason and religion in their own way, selecting a different point in the descent to cross over and begin the ascent towards complex unity, unity in diversity. As image 6.1 shows, not all societies need to fall into the same level of social fragmentation or individualism as experienced in America in order to arrive at postmodernity. The important point is to assure Muslims that the West believes that there are modern alternatives to secularism, and even to the Western version of secularization.

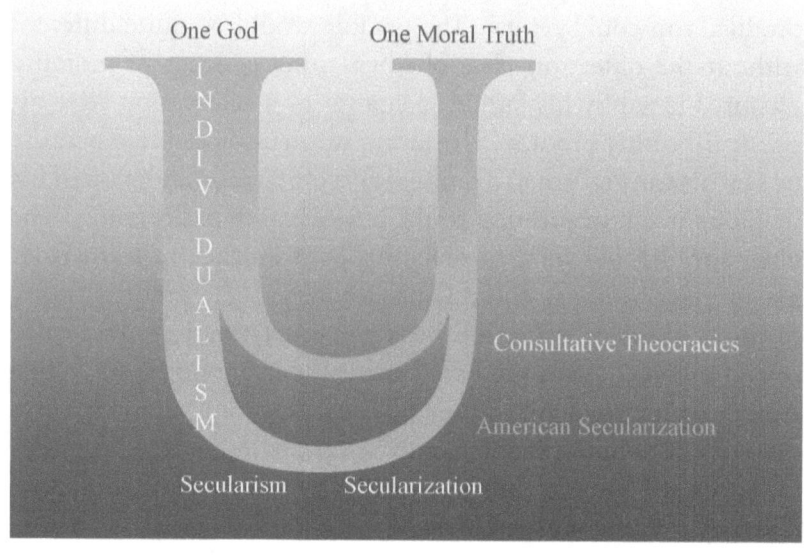

Consultative Secularization

CONSULTATIVE SECULARIZATION

Plato believed that the task of reconciliation was most appropriate for specially trained philosopher kings. There are advantages to a more centralized approach: the underlying structure of society is maintained, while a small subgroup can devote their lives to understanding the intricate disciplines of philosophy and theology. There are fewer individual tragedies under this model because of the advantage of a stronger public spirituality. Public spirituality is rarely experienced in Western countries, and provides a contrast from which both East and West can learn. Muslim scholars and theologians can also benefit by studying the West in order to rationally explain why their religious structure better addresses those needs not politically protected in the West.

There are, however, also serious disadvantages. Centralized political models require a significant level of trust in leaders who may not reflect the diversity of their populations. Further, when leaders lack faith in monotruism or secularization, they will corrupt not only their own lives and the institutions they run, but potentially the entire society. As learned from the fall of Communism, when centralized leadership fails, the fall is devastatingly hard on citizens who were trained not to take initiative, question, or create.

Further, knowing the propensity of power to corrupt, Plato denied the philosopher kings excessive wealth in order to keep them focused on their critical roles as moral and intellectual leaders. But Plato's Republic is not required to convince Muslims of the potential for corruption. Consider Azzam Tamini's summary of Rashid Rida's (1865–1935) views on Islamic corruption:

> Rashid Rida ... suggested that the reason for the backwardness of the ummah lay in the fact that the Muslims had lost the truth of their religion, and that despotic political rulers had encouraged this. "For true Islam involves two things, acceptance of tawhid [creed of monotheism] and shura [consultation] in matters of state, but despotic rulers have tried to make Muslims forget the second by encouraging them to abandon the first.[8]

Rida's articulation of fundamental Islamic principles of mono-theism and consultation is a commitment to secularization—because secularization is a political commitment to an ongoing process of articulating one truth through a process of public consultation. A fascinating example of such progressive consultation and religious reconciliation of minority rights is when the Ayatollah Khomeini's granted Maryam Molkara's request for an official blessing of her desire for male to female reassignment surgery in 1987.

Khomeini responded to Molkara's request by stating that transsexuals had a religious obligation to have the sex change procedure because a person needs a clear sexual identity in order to carry out his or her religious duties. Of note was the fact that Khomeini used Maryam's feelings to justify his conclusion that Maryam should observe all the rites specific to women, including the way they dress. The progressive nature of the Ayatollah's decision is most appreciated by contrasting it with Maryam's mother's reaction, which, consistent with popular opinion, was to refuse to acknowledge or respect Maryam's feelings. Because of her mother's reaction, Maryam waited ten years to receive the gender reassignment surgery. By that time, the state-affiliated religious charity, Imam Khomeini Relief Committee, was paying for transgender operations for many Muslim transsexuals.

Maryam's story lends credence to John Esposito's point in his essay *Islam and Secularism in the Twenty First Century*, that respecting religion is not a step backward. Westerners fear religion because the Western view of a secular modernity keeps the concept of religion stagnant:

> It has artificially compartmentalized religion, doing violence to its nature, and reinforced a static, reified conception of religious traditions rather than revealing their inner dynamic nature.[9]

Abdelwahab El-Affendi, a senior research fellow at the Centre for the Study of Democracy, University of Westminster, in the following quotation from his essay *Rationality of Politics and Politics of Rationality*, articulates the basic principles of Islam, which appear to be quite consistent with the goals of secularization:

The right starting point would have been the basic principles enjoined by Islam: the pursuit of justice and respect for the Law and fundamental values of Islam, which are also basically human and universal in character. Any system which responds to these criteria is the correct one. And it goes without saying that more than one system could do so.[10]

CATHOLIC SECULARIZATION

The Catholic version of secularization is presented here to show that the East and the West are not that different, in that the Catholic version of secularization has more in common with Islamic Secularization, than with secularism. Pope John Paul II's endorsement of the premises of secularization is revealed in this quotation from his Encyclical Letter *Fides and Ratio*:

> It is to be hoped therefore that theologians and philosophers will let themselves be guided by the authority of truth alone so that there will emerge a philosophy consonant with the word of God.[11]

While the Catholic Church believes that reason and faith can and should be reconciled into one truth, they more likely follow this version, consistent with Aquinas' argument in *Summa Theologica*[12] and Pope John Paul II's Encyclical Letter:

1. There is a universal moral truth;

2. Both reason and faith are valid paths to the one truth;

3. Theologians, as experts in both theology and philosophy, should be consulted by individuals as they consider new experiences, and must remain

the final arbitrators in reconciling reason and revelation.

When reviewing Catholic secularization, interesting questions about an arbiter's qualifications arise. Similar restrictions are prescribed by both Plato for his philosopher kings, and by the Catholic Church for priests; neither is permitted to marry or to own property. One difference is that in the Republic women were able to qualify, as the only criterion was the ability to reason, while gender is the primary criterion in the Catholic Church.

Islam and religious America have more in common than either would like to admit: both are experiencing a religious resurgence; both are ambitious, determined, and proud. Once both societies realize that they are united in their belief in secularization, over secularism, opportunities for meaningful collaboration will foster a new era of trust and mutual respect. However, as a condition for this new era to be brought about both societies must get past the animosity between believers and secularists. To this end, politicians and legal professionals must make clear whether they are committed to secularism, secularization, or to closed theocracies, so individuals can adjust their expectations and choices accordingly. To assist in this endeavor, the next Chapter looks at two secular constitutional models and considers how they structurally support secularization versus secularism.

Before doing so, however, a quick reference to polytheistic cultures is worth mentioning. The monotheistic U-shaped plot, while not a mythos of polytheistic cultures, is not necessarily incompatible with them when monotheism is reduced to monotruism because polytheism or pantheism do not necessarily reject the idea of there being one ultimate truth. Further, when the Western world better understands and respects the nature and importance of their own myths, hopefully more respect will be afforded to polytheistic cultures and to the wisdom contained in their myths.

NOTES

1. John Esposito and Azzam Tamini (eds.) Islam and Secularism in the Middle East, (London: Hurst and Company, 2000) 14.

2. Sheikh Salman Islam and Secularism, Islamtoday.com as of August, 2009.

3. Ibid, 5.

4. Ibid, 6.

5. Asghar Ali Engineer "Islam and Secularism" http://www. geocities.com/indiafas/India/islam_&_secularism.htm

6. Northrop Frye, The Secular Scripture, 172.

7. Western Academics "still make assumptions that prevent them from questioning aspects of Western modernity. For example, they call these movements 'reactionary' or 'invented,' making the assumption that Western modernity is not only the standard by which all contemporary developments must be judged, but also the only authentic trajectory for every tradition." Interview, with Talal Asad "Modern power and the reconfiguration of religious traditions" by Saba Mahmood. Stanford Humanities Review, v. 5, n. 1 (http://www.stanford. edu/group/SHR/5-1/text/asad.html

8. Esposito & Tamini, "The Origins of Arab Secularism" 24.

9. Ibid, 11.

10. Ibid, 164.

11. John Paul II, Fides et Ratio, Encyclical Letter, September 15, 1998, http://vatican.va/holy_father/john_paul_ii/encyclicals/documents p. 37.

12. Question 90, Article Four of the Second Part of the Summa, states that law "is nothing else than an ordinance of reason for the common good, made by him who has care of the community, and promulgated."

CHAPTER 7 –
SECULAR CONSTITUTIONS

> Like man, like state
> —Plato

Just as individuals combine reason, religion (or spirituality) with their own personal experiences to arrive at their understanding of right and wrong, so do political states. In addition to their express secular values, governments can be distinguished by the weightings they give to the electorate, the judiciary and the legislature. Liberal democracies favoring secularism can be identified by constitutional principles where institutional reasoning consistently overrides democratic input. Those supporting secularization would more consistently value democratic input.

For example, the judiciary is the state institution that is held most closely accountable to reason by requiring rationally consistent, written decisions that are subject to appeal. Because judges are appointed for life, they are less easily influenced by public sentiment and therefore can more easily adhere to rational principles. Judiciaries with greater independence and power relative to the legislative branches and electorate will naturally lead a society toward secularism because of its appropriate bias towards reasoning. This also occurs because more often than not, the judiciary makes their decisions based on the evidence presented by particular parties, not on the basis of universal theories of human nature or social science. Case law is a bottom up analysis that always starts with the facts.

The elected houses of representatives on the other hand are the practical deal makers, where reason, faith, and experience are all blended together. Legislation, in comparison to court decisions, more often reflects short-term, practical compromises involving many participants, significantly reducing the chances of creating legislation based on consistent rational principles, values, or objectives. But the result is more sensitive to the democratic wishes of citizens because the debates are public and elected officials must continually seek re-election.

Finally, voting, referendums, and citizen's initiatives provide increasingly direct means of incorporating personal religious beliefs and experiences into the law because votes are cast in secret and do not require rational explanations. The ability for referendums to override laws and even constitutional clauses speaks to the level of individual power in a society. While this process is the most democratic means of making decisions, it is clearly not an efficient process and many issues are just too technical and specialized to be properly decided by popular vote.

COMPARING SECULAR CONSTITUTIONS

> When you have an elephant by the hind legs and he is trying to get away, it's best to let him
> —Abraham Lincoln

A constitutional comparison between Canada and the United States reveals that Canada does not have an anti-establishment clause, but ironically Canada has built a more formidable legal wall separating church and state. For instance in 2005, without much public debate, and without the majority of Canadians supporting the position, the federal government passed an amendment declaring same-sex marriage constitutional.[1]

Comparing America's constitutional commitment to "the individual pursuit of happiness", to Canada's "peace, order and good government", might summarize why Canadian elephants don't seem to want to get away as often as their American cousins do. However few Canadians are even aware of their constitutional preamble, so it is proposed that the following constitutional rights outlined in Chart 7.1 below are more likely the source of Canadian "tolerance".

Canada's government has a parliamentary structure and therefore significantly fewer checks and balances than America's Republican model. Canada has greater party discipline, less frequent federal elections (usually); less input into the selection of their judges, and an appointed, not elected, Senate. Furthermore, Canadian citizens have no rights to citizen's initiatives or referendums and their Prime Minister can unilaterally shut down the business of Parliament, through the constitutional right to prorogue Parliament. In summary, Canadians have far fewer democratic opportunities to express their political opinions, informed by their personal experiences and religious beliefs.

This is quite unlike constitutional law in America where individual citizens are asked for their opinions far more frequently, and can even initiate referendums in some states. These referendums are not carefully crafted by the governing party, and they can address constitutional rights, as happened in California in 2008 on the issue of same-sex marriage. The result is that Canadian politicians and administrative bodies when drafting legislation worry more about the Supreme Court than consulting public opinion.

The relative lack of public debate on issues of religious morality should not be mistaken for tolerance in Canada. Just like in America, Canada's conservative party has also moved from a fiscal, to a socially conservative, agenda in the last twenty years. The Canadian struggle is well symbolized by the largely ignored preamble to Canada's Charter, which states: "Whereas Canada is founded upon principles that recognize the supremacy of God and the rule of law." While a simple reference to God could be interpreted as just an historical reference and hence just a throwaway line, the phrase "supremacy of God" suggests something more profound was intended to be preserved.

The clear contradiction between constitutional supremacy and the "supremacy of God" can be reconciled in a pluralistic society by interpreting God metaphorically as a unifying faith in one truth, whilst still acknowledging the value in diversity. In other words, Canada could be a society committed to secularization. But this has not been the path taken by the Supreme Court, which has been demonstrating a commitment toward Postmodern Secularism and its express commitment to celebrating diversity as the end goal of Canadian culture.

Canada heavily leans towards Postmodern Secularism by limiting the number and ways for citizens with religious beliefs to affect the selection of judges, senators, members of Parliament, and thus Canadian law, as well as its express commitments to Postmodern Secularism's value of promoting and enhancing diversity as a Canadian value. How these differences play out practically is more fully explored in the next chapter which examines the secular obligations of Canadian school boards in deciding whether books on same-sex marriage are appropriate materials for school curriculums.

CHART 7.1 - Comparing Secular Constitutions		
Constitutional Dimension	← Secularization	Secularism →
	United States	Canada
Separating Church and State	First Amendment, 1791 "Congress shall make no law respecting an establishment of religion, or prohibiting the free exercise thereof;	Constitution Act, 1982 S.1 "Guarantees rights and freedoms set out in it subject only to such *reasonable* limits prescribed by law as can be *demonstrably justified* in a free and democratic society"
Judicial Review	Judicial Supremacy controversial since *Marbury* v. *Madison* in 1803 Intermittent periods of activism most clearly on fundamental rights. State constitutions subject to citizen initiatives.	Constitutional Supremacy - Parliamentary Supremacy barely retained through s.33 override. "Trend towards a liberal judicial philosophy especially in matters relating to abortion, feminist causes, sexual orientation and protecting the rights of accused"[2]
Supreme Court Appointments	Nominated by President Public Confirmation Hearings conducted by Senate, confirmed with simple majority.	Small advisory group with significant legal expertise make recommendations to Prime Minister who then makes the appointment.
Reference Questions	Not allowed.	Allowed under Supreme Court Act and frequently used.

Legislative overrides to Case law	Allowed by 2/3 of Congress & then must be ratified by States. Fairly common occurrence.	Sec 33 - Parliament can only override but must be continually renewed every 5 years. Only used once since 1985.
Citizen's Initiatives	Most states with minimum percent of electorate (8% in California) can amend constitutions by referendum with simple majority. Used quite often.	No right to citizen initiatives at either Federal or Provincial levels.
Postmodern Diversity	No References.	S. 27 "This Charter shall be interpreted in a manner consistent with the preservation and enhancement of the multi-cultural heritage of Canadians".
Partisan closure of House	No ability.	Prime Minister of a minority government can prorogue Parliament

RELIGIOUS JUDGES AND ELECTED OFFICIALS

Rational Secularists prefer that judges and elected politicians not have religious beliefs because they personally do not believe that reason and faith can be reconciled. To be fair, not many believers have done this well or do so publicly. Secularization supports the view that religious beliefs provide an additional perspective to a legal analysis, but requires judges express their opinions in rational terms. A key difference between the mature secular state of America, versus Iraq in 2005 is that American citizens (and judges) are completely free to choose their religious beliefs and therefore far less likely to be influenced by them in their decisions.

George W. Bush was likely hoping that Harriet Miers would be able to strike this balance when he recommended her for appointment to the U.S. Supreme Court. Because Miers failed to convince secularists of her legal expertise, Bush had to withdraw her nomination for lack of support. It is important to distinguish this result from Postmodern Secularism, which would have rejected strong monotheistic religious views outright, regardless of Mier's legal competency because monotruistic values directly compete with ensuring diversity. Rational Secularists which would reject religious beliefs as indications of irrational thinking. The following review of American jurisprudence shows how the bench found the principles of secularization, by treading the very fine line required by the dual nature of Romantic Secularism's first amendment.

Ronald Reagan was the first American president to make use of judicial appointments to fight secularism in the early 1980s. Not long thereafter, a shift on the bench in favor of secularization was noticeable. For example, the U.S. Supreme Court, in a 5–4 decision in *Mueller v. Allen* (1983), reasoned that because an income tax deduction was granted *directly to parents* who had both religious and secular school choices, a Minnesota tax policy did not constitute funding churches or establishing religion.

Further, the *Zelman v. Simmons-Harris* (2002) case advanced the "true private choice" argument as the rationale for allowing religious schools to participate in Ohio's voucher program for low-income parents. This decision reflects a commitment to secularization because it trusts citizens to reconcile their beliefs in the context of real life choices. Voucher programs did not amount to presidential, legislative or court-mandated beliefs, and thus did not trip the prohibition against the "establishment of a religion". In this case, it was critical for the court that there were many religious and secular options available to parents.

The "true private choice" argument is a fine line to tread because a legal decision can outlive the broad range of secular and religious options available at the time of the decision, especially if communities start to segregate along secular lines. However, what is fascinating about the rationale is that if religious schools are to continue to receive voucher funding, they must ensure the community balance is maintained, requiring that secularists and believers learn to live together. This constitutional balance is consistent with Habermas' call for direct personal interaction on ethical issues and simultaneously with Jefferson's rationale that individuals are only morally accountable to their God directly. Finally it is also consistent with the Biblical call to treat your neighbor as you would like to be treated yourself.

In summary, judges with religious beliefs are important to the secularization cause in that if they believe they can (and do) reconcile their religious beliefs with reason; they are more apt to ensure that the constitution allows citizens to do the same. It is no different than believing that diversity of race will improve the overall quality of decision making on the bench because it expands the diversity of experiences and perspectives that can be brought into the collective decision-making process. The Supreme Court's reasoning in the Anti-establishment Clause cases appears to have reached that delicate balance.

The danger in this approach is that if a religious judge does not respect the distinction between secularization and a theocracy, failing to relinquish the second and third exclusive commitments of monotheism, then religious beliefs should be seen as a detrimental quality for serving on the bench. Overly political appointments, on either side, run the risk of putting the American judicial system out of balance.

In Canada, by way of contrast, reconciliation of cultural diversity is not expected of parents, but is rather to occur within public schools. This objective was articulated by the Canadian government in 1999 when responding to a charge that the Canadian constitution violated the United Nation's International

Covenant on Civil and Political Rights by not extending its historical constitutional obligation from 1867 to fund separate catholic schools to other private religious schools.

The federal government argued that public schools are a "rational means of fostering social cohesion and respect for religious and other differences. Schools are better able to teach common understanding and shared values if they are less homogeneous." Furthermore, they argued that "extending public school funding rights to private religious schools would undermine this ability and may result in a significant increase in the number and kind of private schools."[3]

Even though the U.N. Human Rights Committee found that the Canadian constitution was discriminatory in 1999 and reiterated its conclusion in 2005, there is insufficient political will to change the situation. Indeed, in Ontario, Canada's most populous province, since 2000 there have been two unsuccessful political campaigns to secure funding of private religious schools through tax credits.

Examined side by side, the Canadian and American approaches raise the interesting question of whether children, parents, or judges are best able to reconcile the conflicts between reason and faith. It would be of interest to determine if children raised in Canadian public schools were more likely to believe that reason and religions can be reconciled, or whether they become moral relativists. As Canada has a higher incidence of atheism, it is likely the latter.

SECULARIZATION AND THE OFFICE OF THE PRESIDENT

In the US case *Hein v. Freedom from Religion Foundation* (2007), the constitutionality of the White House Office of Faith-based and Community Initiatives was challenged for violating the Anti-establishment clause of the First Amendment. The case was defeated on the basis that taxpayer standing was limited to challenging the legislative branch, not the executive branch.

This judicial result was unfortunate because if the allegations were true, as the Office name suggests, the lack of state neutrality violates the spirit of secularization. Reason and faith should be reconciled, but never by offices of the state. President Obama was elected, largely because he personified secularization by striking the delicate balance between his rational legal training and respect for religion, and it shows in his happy marriage and family life. Individuals, like states, seek to find this balance of body, mind and spirit. This balance eluded George W. Bush and Bill Clinton for very different reasons. Secularization, as embodied by Obama, is back in the White House, but he is in serious jeopardy of being brought down by the extremists on either side of the wall if he cannot articulate the principles that guide his judgment.

NOTES

1. Same-sex marriage polls conducted by CROP, Inc., found in 1992 that 35.8 percent of Canadians totally or somewhat agreed with the question "Society should regard people of the same sex who live together as being the same as a married couple." Between November 2002 and April 2005, support for same-sex marriage rarely exceeded 50 percent. David Pettinicchio University of Washington Do Canadians Want Same-Sex Marriage Legislation?: The Role of Parties, Interest Groups and Public Opinion in the Enactment of the Civil Marriage Act presented at the annual meeting of the American Sociological Association, Montreal, Quebec, Canada, Aug 11, 2006. Online <PDF> p3. 2009-07-29 http://www.allacademic.com/meta/p103645_index.html.

2. "Judicial Power and Canadian Democracy" in Paul Howe and Peter H. Russel (eds.), Judicial Politics in Canada, Patterns and Trends (Toronto: McGill-Queens University Press, 2001) 21.

3. International Covenant on Political and Civil Rights, Communication N° 694/1996 : Canada. 05/11/99 , para 4.4.4 http://www.unhchr.ch/tbs/doc.nsf/0/b3bfc541589cc3 0f802568690052e5d6

Chapter 8 –
Canada's Postmodern
Secularism

> The Americans combine the notions of religion and liberty so
> intimately in their minds that it is impossible to make them
> conceive of one without the other.
> —Alexis De Tocqueville

That so many Americans classify Canada as a socialist country
is perplexing to Canadians, who are quite committed to their
capitalist economy. Canadians simply believe that well-funded
public schools and universal health care contribute to a vibrant
free-market economy. However, the classification makes more
sense when Canadians appreciate that the American fight against
communism was just as much about fighting for the freedom
of religion, as it was about fighting for a free market. It is not a
coincidence that the religious motto "In God we Trust" found on
American currency, was adopted in 1956 just after the Warsaw
Pact was signed.

Canada did not have a strong secular commitment to liberty
and so it avoided direct participation in the Cold War. Canada
is too small for big enemies and so Canada's most pressing

political issue is, and has always been, the French/English divide. Consequently for Canadian school children, the "us versus them" is most clearly pronounced in the Protestant versus Catholic school systems which are constitutionally guaranteed to preserve French culture. Canada's divide is internal, America's is external. This historical difference foreshadowed Canada's lead role in advancing Postmodern Secularism's commitment to diversity—that and Canada's desire to distinguish itself from its rather imposing and yet disinterested neighbor to the south.

The aim of this Chapter is to show how the values of Postmodern Secularism play out in real life situations and has the effect of excluding from public discussion, the values of monotruists in Canada. For this purpose, the case *Chamberlain v. Surrey School District* is reviewed because it contains the Canadian Supreme Court's articulation of its commitment to Postmodern Secularism. The *Chamberlain* case is the first case where the Supreme Court defines "secular" and demonstrates the court's willingness to cross the line into the realm of private beliefs in order to protect the feelings, and not just the constitutional rights, of minority groups. The effect is that *Chamberlain* almost requires state institutions such as the courts and school boards, to reconcile differences in moral beliefs in favor of diverse minorities, as opposed to letting individuals reconcile these differences for themselves, or through democratic means.

As Justice Gonthier attempted to warn his colleagues in his dissenting opinion, the *Chamberlain* decision does not rest on assumptions consistent with liberal democracies. The case is an example of the unconscious pull of monotruism on those who claim to hold diversity as their moral standard. Monotruism led the court to strongly suggest a clear winner instead of using the legal framework to conclude that matters of belief are beyond the jurisdiction of the state and the education system, in a secular society.

THE FACTS IN CHAMBERLAIN

Following a heated public debate, the elected School Board in Surrey, British Columbia passed a resolution not to approve three books depicting same-sex parental families for use as "learning resources" for kindergarten and grade one levels. Following the debate, the board and superintendent distributed a directive that clarified their position:

> There has been extensive media coverage regarding recent board motions on learning resources and sexual orientation. Let there be no confusion with regard to the District's expectation in terms of how we treat the matter of sexual orientation. The District will not accept any action of intolerance or discriminatory treatment of students, staff, or parents on the basis of their sexual orientation. Administrative officers must be vigilant in their responsibility and must confront instances of intolerance to ensure that they cease and that appropriate action results.[1]

Despite the clarification of its position, the Board's resolution was appealed, ultimately to the Supreme Court of Canada, on the basis that it violated the following sections (76) of the School Act which read:

> (1) All schools and Provincial schools must be conducted on strictly secular and non-sectarian principles.
>
> (2) The highest morality must be inculcated, but no religious dogma or creed is to be taught in a school or Provincial school.[2]

The Supreme Court granted the appeal and set aside the board's decision. The Court provided the following judgment:

In summary, the Act's requirement of strict secularism means that the board must conduct its deliberations on all matters, including the approval of supplementary resources, in a manner that respects the views of all members of the school community. It cannot prefer the religious views of some people in its district to the views of other segments of the community. Nor can it appeal to views that deny the equal validity of the lawful lifestyles of some in the school community. The board must act in a way that promotes respect and tolerance for all the diverse groups that it represents and serves.[3]

JUDICIAL REVIEW, NOT PUBLIC RECONCILIATION

The first point, consistent with the findings in Chapter Seven, demonstrates how the Canadian governmental structure resulted in the court having little hesitation in intervening in a decision of an elected board that was specifically charged by an elected legislature with consulting with parents in order to make a decision that reflected community values. This intervention was justified despite there being no allegation of breached constitutional rights, and the majority of the community supporting the decision. The majority of the members of the Supreme Court justified the supervision of the board's decision on the following grounds:

> The board is a political body and a proxy for parents and local community members in making decisions and has been granted a degree of choice on which the legislature has conferred a circumscribed role in approving books. However, the deference that might be warranted

by these factors, standing alone, is undercut by clear commitment of the legislature and the Minister to promoting tolerance and respect for diversity. These goals, touching on fundamental human rights and constitutional values, suggest the legislature intended a relatively robust level of court supervision.[4]

THE CANADIAN SUPREME COURT INTERPRETS "SECULAR PRINCIPLES"

The Supreme Court's decision was reached in large part because the word "secular" is so poorly defined in both legal and academic literature. At its simplest, "secular" means "not under religious control", because at one time the politically established church controlled many public institutions. Therefore, when an institution such as a university or a hospital was no longer under the control of the church, it was deemed to be secular.

When this concept is applied to governments and when the governments must *simultaneously* respect their citizens' freedom of religion, it becomes necessary to further refine the term "secular", by excising from state jurisdiction the private sphere of spiritual beliefs. In the historical context of the British Columbia School Act, "secular" meant not to prefer one Christian denomination over another. This paradox of protecting, even while containing religious beliefs, forces the state to be neutral towards religion and to limit its moral authority to the public, material realm where reason, the universal language, can legitimately prevail through persuasion. This abstract line between public and private is commonly defined by distinguishing between beliefs and actions; it is less frequently defined by distinguishing between spiritual and material worlds. It is maintained to ensure that officers of the state are not imposing their private beliefs on citizens through policies or funding decisions.

Until recently, the Canadian courts have been generous in offering protection to the practice of religion, going even beyond the right to hold certain beliefs, by allowing certain public actions, unless harm was caused:

> Freedom means that, subject to such limitations as are necessary to protect public safety, order, health, or morals or the fundamental rights and freedoms of others, no one is to be forced to act in a way contrary to his beliefs or his conscience.[5]

The Court's treatment of the term *secular* started off well, acknowledging that it is the officers of the state, not individual citizens, who are required to leave their personal beliefs at the boardroom door:

> The Act's insistence on strict secularism does not mean that religious concerns have no place in the deliberations and decisions of the board. Board members are entitled, and indeed required, to bring the views of the parents and communities they represent to the deliberation process. Because religion plays an important role in the life of many communities, these views will often be motivated by religious concerns. Religion is an integral aspect of people's lives, and cannot be left at the boardroom door.[6]

The court failed to decide whether secularism required the state to respect the jurisdiction of private beliefs. Although the issue was the conflicting *beliefs* about the ideal family unit, religious freedom was quickly acknowledged, but then dismissed. Instead, the Court decided the case as if it was considering a section 15 equality violation:

> What secularism does rule out, however, is any attempt to use the religious views of one part of

the community to exclude from consideration
the values of other members of the community.

This is particularly disturbing because the decision doesn't
discuss any evidence of discriminatory actions of excluding
"….from consideration the values of other members of the
community." The wording implies that religious parents were
objecting to same-sex parents having their views represented
at the board or, denying their right to participate in the board
hearings. The objection was the presentation of books to young
children on a spiritual matter because it was believed that a key
aspect of religious freedom included the right to oversee the
education of children's spiritual beliefs. Hence the desire for the
issue to be removed out of the school, in keeping with respect for
the private/public line that is critical to the constitutional right
to freedom of conscience and religion.

Had this definition of secularism been considered by the
court, it would have realized that the board was actually making
their decision by trying to respect the underpinnings of Romantic
Secularism, whereby the state respects the realm of private beliefs.
Evidence of this approach was contained in the superintendent's
memo to the board:

> I was also concerned that the right of parents to
> be the primary educators in the development of
> attitudes and values of Kindergarten and Grade
> One children be maintained. I found it difficult to
> conclude that by approving the Three Books for
> Kindergarten and Grade One, the school would
> be providing a supportive role and maintaining a
> partnership between home and school.[7]

Even though the court determined that the board made its
decision based on the superintendent's recommendations and
comments, and not on the basis of religious parent's concerns it
still decided the Board was not acting in a secular manner:

Although the final decision was the board's and not the superintendent's, the above passage appears to express the concerns on which the board relied.

The majority decision in Chamberlain implies that the term "secular" means ensuring diversity, not ensuring state neutrality, when it comes to spiritual values:

What the Superintendent and the Board did not consider is as telling as what they did consider. The Superintendent's statement does not refer to the absence of restriction on the curriculum's direction to discuss different family types. It does not refer to the emphasis in the School Act and curriculum on tolerance, respect, inclusion and understanding of social and family diversity. *And it does not refer to the secular nature of the public school system and its mandate to provide a nurturing and validating learning experience for all children, regardless of the types of families they come from.* [Emphasis added].[8]

By trying to provide "validating learning experiences", as opposed to protecting individuals against discriminatory legislation or actions, the state loses its neutrality. With no evidence of a lack of respect, with only a disagreement over the appropriate forum for a discussion on values, the Chief Justice still concluded:

I conclude that the Board's decision is unreasonable. It failed to proceed as required by the secular mandate of the School Act by letting the religious views of a certain part of the community trump the need to show equal respect for the values of other members of the community.[9]

These errors went to the heart of the Board's decision. It is suggested that rejection of the materials did not materially lessen the opportunities for teaching and enforcing tolerance in the classroom, and therefore is of no great moment. Yet to the appellants, it is a matter of importance. The last word—indeed the only word that counts—is the word of the legislature and the curriculum. It stresses tolerance and inclusion, and places high importance on discussion and understanding of all family groups. The Board's rejection of these values must be seen as serious.[10]

The last word in a legal system, as the Chief Justice successfully argued when intervening in the case in the first place, is the Constitution. There was far more evidence that the right to religious freedom was appropriately upheld than there was evidence of any individual's right to equality being violated. If "secular" means, as the case law on freedom of religion has made clear, that the board must respect the distinction between private beliefs and public actions, then the board's decision was completely reasonable and consistent with the objective of the school not being in a position of endorsing one view at the expense of another. It was also consistent with the UN Declaration and case law identifying the education of children as being a fundamental aspect of religious freedom.

Coming to such a conclusion first would have precluded any consideration of ensuring diversity of *beliefs*. Discriminating against people is unconstitutional; disagreeing with their beliefs or conduct is not. The majority opinion of the court was able to overstep this problem by implying discriminatory action occurred without clearly labeling it. The wording of the decision implies that the board never seriously considered the books, solely because of the religious dissent. Further, indicative of a judiciary committed to Postmodern Secularism is the lack of meaningful feedback to the board on how to reconcile the legitimate differences of opinion within its community. By failing to articulate a clear definition of "secular", the court is free to use Romantic Secularism or Postmodern Secularism, as it wishes, issue by issue.

While confusion over the word "secularism" is widespread, the error could have been avoided if the case had been classified as a legitimate conflict between equality, and freedom of religion, consistent with Justice Gonthier's dissenting opinion. In his dissent, Justice Gonthier points out the lack of evidence for discriminatory or disrespectful behavior, but points to a legitimate conflict:

> Adults in Canadian society who think that homosexual behavior is immoral can still be staunchly committed to nondiscrimination. In the case at bar, there is, in my view, no evidence that the parents who felt that the Three Books were inappropriate for five- and six-year-old children fostered discrimination against persons in any way. Many persons, religious and not, justify this distinction by drawing a line, reflected in the passages above, between beliefs held about persons and beliefs held about the conduct of persons.[11]

Therefore, Justice Gonthier more readily admits that there is a legitimate conflict to the balanced:

> [L]language espousing "tolerance" ought not be employed as a cloak for the means of obliterating disagreement ... In my view, the relationship between s. 2 and s. 15 of the Charter, in a truly

free society, must permit persons who respect the
fundamental and inherent dignity of others and
who do not discriminate, to still disagree with
others and even disapprove of the conduct or
beliefs of others. Otherwise, claims for "respect" or
"recognition" or "tolerance," where such language
becomes a constitutionally mandated proxy for
"acceptance," tend to obliterate disagreement.[12]

When "secular" is used as a proxy for ensuring diversity,
it is reasonable to conclude that the board failed to honor
the requirements of the Act. Secular cannot mean ensuring
universal commitment to promoting diversity, because that
conclusion would completely erode the right to freedom of
conscience and would exclude religious diversity. It is especially
egregious to monotheistic religious beliefs not because they are
imperialistic, but instead, because they believe in one moral
truth—monotruism. While not directly linking his comments to
the definition of secular, Gonthier makes the same point and
concludes that private beliefs are beyond legal jurisdiction:

Can s. 15 be used to eliminate beliefs, whether
popular or unpopular? In a society committed to
liberal values and robust pluralism, the answer to
all of these questions must be in the negative.[13]

Secularization and Gonthier's dissent are consistent with
Charles Taylor's definition of "open secularism":

The State is sovereign in its fields of jurisdiction.
On the other hand, the State must also be neutral
from the standpoint of religions and other deep-
seated convictions. It must neither favour nor
put at a disadvantage any of them. In order to
recognize the equal value of all citizens, the State
must be able, in principle, to justify to each

citizen each of the decisions that it makes, which
it cannot do if it favours a specific conception of
the world and of good.[14]

Gonthier's final quotation further reflects someone who,
because he acknowledges that a reconciliation of diversity has to
be done by someone, questions whether it is fair to expect this of
young children.

> Very young children cannot assess competing
> moral views about homosexual relationships on
> their own. It is not in their best interest that they,
> or their parents, be placed in the predicament
> of having divergent moral lessons over sensitive
> and controversial issues taught at school and at
> home.[15]

If the School Act supported secularization, it would ensure
that all citizens were given equal opportunity to express their
beliefs in the proper forum, demonstrating respectful ways to
disagree and the fairest way to make decisions in the meanwhile.
Diversity of beliefs would not, however, be celebrated for its
own sake but rather would be acknowledged and presented as
a collective responsibility to search for the reasons why moral
opinions might legitimately differ. It is a good opportunity to
teach the difference between logos and mythos, and that there is
still much for science to discover about our human nature that
underpins morality. This approach would support communities
and not divide them. Citizens can live without certainty and
agreement, but they cannot live without the hope of it.

BIAS AGAINST RELIGION

Bias is the belief in the superiority of one view by failing to
acknowledge a legitimate conflict and therein assigning cynical
motivations to those who do not agree with an 'obvious' moral

truth, and thereby justifying coercion. This was done when the court assumed that rationally based *beliefs* were superior to religiously based *beliefs*. Both sides have unproven beliefs about the ideal family structure—one derived through personal experience, the other through religion—neither based on conclusive scientific evidence.

In the face of disagreement, the liberal temperament should assume positive, albeit inarticulate, motives. It is possible that religion reflects a truth that reason has not yet been able to appreciate, and therefore cannot yet be expressed rationally. A recent example includes the discovery of the hormone oxytocin released during sexual intercourse. It has a significant bonding influence on women and helps to explain the religious double standard on female sexuality. This discovery may explain such a custom as a protective, not a punitive, restriction merely rationalizing patriarchal privilege.

Another example of religion containing wisdom that reason has been very slow to appreciate is fasting. Romanticism has encouraged us to respect our sentiments and sensations as the highest truth, but clearly our current obesity problem is demonstrating that senses can be equally tyrannical. There is wisdom in every religion's requirement for some type of fasting as a means of learning how to discipline our appetites for maximum well-being. Our ability to reason is not always superior to religion. Lawyers and judges would naturally find this bias difficult to admit but need to remain wary of putting governmental structures out of balance by not respecting their jurisdictional boundaries.

NOTES

1. Chamberlain, para 101.

2. Revised Statutes of British Columbia 1996, Chapter 412.

3. Chamberlain, para 25.

4. Ibid, para 14.

5. Big Drug Mart, supra note lxxiii.

6. Chamberlain, para 19.

7. Ibid, para 48.

8. Ibid, para 49.

9. Ibid, para 71.

10. Ibid, para 72.

11. Ibid, para 127.

12. Ibid, (Gonthier, J., dissenting) para 134.

13. Ibid, para 128.

14. Gerard Bouchard & Charles Taylor, Building the Future, A Time for Reconciliation Report Quebec Religious Accommodations Report. http://www.accommodements. qc.ca/documentation/rapports/rapport-final-integral-en.pdf

15. Chamberlain, para 52.

CHAPTER 9 –
AMERICA UNITED

The greatness of America lies not in being more enlightened than any other nation, but rather in her ability to repair her faults.
—Alexis de Tocqueville

HEALTH CARE REFORM

United under one God
—American Health care Protestor

LEBANON, Pa. — They got up before dawn in large numbers with angry signs and American flag T-shirts, and many were seething with frustration at issues that went far beyond overhauling health care. More than 1,000 people showed up here Tuesday morning in this largely Republican town in central Pennsylvania for a town-hall-style meeting with Senator Arlen Spector.

"This is about the dismantling of this country," Katy Abram, 35, said forcefully to Mr. Specter, drawing one of the most prolonged rounds of applause. "We don't want this country to turn into Russia."

Standing two feet from the senator, Craig Anthony Miller, 59, shouted, "You are trampling on our Constitution!" A half-dozen security people quickly swarmed but refrained from touching him as Mr. Specter, raising his voice, said sternly, "Wait a minute! Wait a minute!" He said the man had the right to leave.

Mr. Miller, shaking, stood his ground. He said he was furious that the senator's staff had limited the questioning. "One day," he said to loud applause, "God is going to stand before you, and he's going to judge you!"[1]

Angry Republicans dumbfounded Democrats with their strident rejection of publicly funded health care in the summer of 2009. Senator John McCain said that President Obama's efforts to reform health care have sparked a peaceful revolt in America. "I've seen involvement and engagement on the part of Americans that I have never seen the likes of which before" said McCain at a town hall in Phoenix.[2] For the second time in less than a year, McCain was urging the unruly Republican crowd to remain respectful and to seek constructive, pro-private sector compromises. And once again, Democrats were frustrated with the lack of meaningful debate, exaggerated accusations of death panels and turning America into a communist country, not to mention more preaching about uniting the country under one God. How does one respond rationally to such allegations? The first step is to understand that the Republican Party is composed of three main factions: Libertarians, social conservatives, and neoconservatives.

UNDERSTANDING THE REPUBLICAN ALLIANCE

When Paul Weyrich founded the Heritage Foundation in 1976, he did so to promote pro-business, libertarian policies on taxation and regulation. He then recruited independent religious leaders to join the Republican Party on the basis of their mutual interest in keeping the federal government small. In the days of the Cold War, this was a natural alliance because communism attacked both religion and capitalism. This alliance became known as fusionism, but it was not an equal partnership because libertarian values dominated, especially once the neoconservatives joined in the 1980's during the Reagan administration.

This political/religious alliance has resulted in considerable cross-pollination in the last forty years. Churches started to be managed like large corporations, and Christian values were used to motivate believers to vote for pro-business policies. The alliance with big business granted believers new status, countering the social indignity of being dismissed as opiate-addicted masses unable to keep up with modernity. The fusionist movement peaked under the Reagan administration, and continued under George H. Bush.

As previously mentioned, Peter Berger argued that the human need for certainty is a primary cause for the current resurgence of religion. The following quotation by Erik Heubeck responds to Berger's claim. By way of introduction, Heubeck was a member of the Free Congress Federation, one of Paul Weyrich's social conservative think tanks. Heubeck and Weyrich were reconsidering the merits of the strategic alliance with the Republican Party after the senate failed to impeach Clinton in 1999. Their movement was demoralized and the following quotation relates to Heubeck's new strategy designed to correct past mistakes:

> We must make it clear that we are seceding from popular culture not because we are unable to cope with modern life, but because we are superior to modern life. We understand popular culture—we get it—we simply find it empty and meaningless.[3]

The thesis of *Secular Hope* is that the religious right has a profound, if inarticulate, understanding of how secularization combines hope and objective truth together in a way that can more effectively politically unite diverse people than can the cold logic of skepticism. Heubeck continued:

> Civilization means, in part, the mores and inherited traditions that encourage self-restraint and consideration for other individuals, as well as an appreciation for objective truth, in a way that is sustainable and in harmony with our essential human nature.

Heubeck wanted to get back to his religious roots and understood that a commitment to truth was critical to personal and cultural transcendence, but he had to find a simple way to express these complex ideas:

> We must reframe this struggle as a moral struggle, as a transcendent struggle, as a struggle between good and evil. And we must be prepared to explain why this is so. We must provide the evidence needed to prove this using images and simple terms.

JANE JACOB'S MONSTROUS HYBRIDS

The common thread that binds the Republican Party, probably more apparent to non-Americans, is that America's modern identity was largely formed by the Cold War. This is an identity that America desperately needs to transcend. Jane Jacobs, an American-born Canadian, wrote a book entitled *Systems of Survival,* in which she explains why the fusion movement cannot be good for America, or for any government. In her book, Jacobs demonstrates that business and science, as opposed to government and religion, work on entirely different ethical foundations and moral systems that should never be mixed.

Jacobs warned that when governments run economies (communism) or governments are run like businesses by privatizing government sectors, or churches are run like businesses, the moral systems cannot function properly and corruption and collapse will be the result. The never-ending religious scandals that plague religious leaders of super-sized congregations support Jacobs' theory well. Jacobs called such organizations "monstrous hybrids" and she used the Soviet Union as the classic example of why monstrous hybrids cannot work. Jacobs was correct in predicting that corruption would continue in Russia long past the fall of the Iron Curtain because it takes generations to reestablish the trust and moral basis necessary to run an efficient economy.

Erik Heubeck understood the negative consequences of the alliance of social conservatives with Libertarians and realized the nature of his "monstrous hybrid":

> Being conservative has come to mean nothing more nuanced than holding the belief that every man has the inalienable right to make as much money as he possibly can. True traditionalist conservatives are now seen as oddities in the movement who must be tolerated, or even silenced

in order that the movement appears credible in the eyes of the leftist guardians of good taste.

But the New Traditionalist movement must be willing to lose allies among the libertarians we brought on board the post-war conservative coalition. While our movement is not anti-freedom, and the practical effect of our ultimate ascendancy to political power (should that happen) would be an increase in political freedom for Americans, we choose not to make a fetish of political freedom.

The ontological libertarians make their arguments in terms that the perfectly happy life is a life free from all restraint. The use of these arguments has been a convenient way to achieve some of the short-term goals of conservatives, because this argument is presented in ontological terms acceptable to the Left—but it has been disastrous to American society. It was an alluring temptation that should have been resisted. It has reaffirmed the world-view of the leftist, which holds the unbridled ego at its center. We have undermined the foundation of any resistance to the Left based on the promotion of a fundamentally different world-view. This devil's bargain has therefore helped to perpetuate the decimation of traditional American culture, with its accumulated wisdom and mores and traditions of self-restraint, which is the basis for any hope of a truly workable political freedom.

While the leaders of the religious right might have understood the consequences of their bargain with the Devil, unfortunately the only other partner was the neo-conservatives. And then Bush got elected.

By 2000 the power dynamic within the Republican Party had changed, largely due to the Bill Clinton impeachment process in 1999. Consequently, George W. Bush was elected mainly on the basis of his moral character as a devout, practicing Christian. The Bush/Cheney ticket reflected the new monstrous hybrid that could not have been worse for responding to the events of 9/11. The results were disastrous. The ticket's legacy was a bloated government that sought to put the church back into the state domestically, while fighting a war to take the mosque out of the state internationally, all eagerly fuelled by the neo-conservative penchant for war. By the 2006 mid-term elections, libertarian states were quickly leaving their alliance with Bush's evangelicals and Bush was reversing many of Cheney's policies, but it was too late.

In 2008 McCain's choice of Sarah Palin as a running mate only continued to alienate the more erudite libertarians, who readily gave their support to Obama. In early 2009, the corporate bailouts were not enough to cause libertarians to switch but Obama's popularity dropped like a rock with Libertarians over health care. Here is how one Libertarian expressed their dilemma:

> Whatever team is more likely to stay out of my pocket and tries not to punish performance (as much) will get my vote. That's why I continue to support "fusionism," the coalition between conservatives and libertarians. In short, the accretion of state power in economic matters is much more serious to me than concerns about the renaissance of the moral majority. I'd rather have a President with quaint views on sexuality and drug use than a Fabian Socialist with a trillion-dollar credit card.[4]

What is most important to understand is that libertarians and neo-conservatives are both very small groups that are geographically dispersed, in proportion to the religious right—who are far easier to organize on Election Day. When the Democrats learn how to respect and acknowledge the best qualities of the religious right, they will crack open the destructive alliance of interests based on fear and greed.

WHERE HOPE WAS LOST

Jane Jacobs further explained, in *Systems of Survival,* that public sectors should not be turned into businesses because they were inherently unprofitable if done well. One such sector is education. American patriots, by narrowly defining America as the champion of capitalism and individualism are inadvertently eroding the very foundation of a healthy democracy—educated citizens.

Peter Berger argued that secularization was a failure because he assumed that transcendence was an entirely private matter. "The critique of secularity common to all the resurgent movements is that human existence bereft of transcendence is an impoverished and finally untenable condition." Berger failed to consider the political and economic changes that gutted the secular transcendental institutions that preceded the religious resurgence. Religions do not, in ordinary circumstances, have a monopoly on transcendence, but they do when quality education and legal justice is not available. The rise in religious beliefs closely parallels the rise in private school tuition fees.

Average tuition fees at American private institutions rose by 4.3 percent in 2009–10, the smallest increase since 1972–73. "To an unprecedented degree, students and families are concerned about affording the college of their choice."[5] Between 1982 and 2007, college tuition and fees rose three times as fast as median family income, in constant dollars. Hope of personal transcendence through education has been consistently eroding for thirty-seven years.

Personal transcendence cannot happen in isolation. Education used to be the institution that provided the certainty that talent and hard work would be rewarded. The lower tuition fees at community colleges have been attracting more and more students, to the point that some colleges cannot accommodate all the applicants. Miami-Dade Community College in Florida, America's largest with about 164,000 students, expects to turn away 5,000 students in 2009.[6] In the face of rising tuition fees and predatory lending, hope in transcendence through education has faded. It has been replaced by the lottery of professional sports, the 'modeling' industry, drug dealing and reality TV appearances.

Given Canada's better funding of public education and regulated tuition fees, the Canadian trend is not as severe. However, the annual rise in tuition fees for undergraduate students was still averaging four percent since 2000 (consistently above the rate of inflation) after annual increases of 10 percent throughout the 1990's. The most disturbing pattern was found when tuition fees were deregulated in the 1990's:

> Tuition fees for professional programs in Ontario's universities soared during the late 1990s, nearly quadrupling in the case of medicine and almost tripling for law. A new study has found that these big jumps were associated with substantial changes in the likelihood that students from different socio-economic backgrounds would enroll in medicine, law or dentistry programs.[7]

The response to rising tuition fees has always been a chorus of corresponding increases in student aid and scholarships. However, these increases are rarely matched on a percentage basis to the increases in tuition, and because they are only offered to a small portion of the students, it further erodes the students' ability to choose their own education. The evidence suggests that equality rights are seriously compromised in such a system.

Higher tuition fees, in both Canada and the United States, were the direct result of lowering the top marginal tax rates. In the United States, rates dropped from 70 percent in 1980 to 50 percent in 1982, reflecting Reagan's first term in office. They dropped again by a staggering 22 percent by 1988, for a low of 28 percent. During the Clinton administration the rate went back up to 39.6 percent in 1993, remaining relatively unchanged until 2003. George W. Bush lowered it again to 35 percent, where it remains to the present day.[8] In Canada, the pattern was generally the same, but in the early 1990's, Canada realized that this was unsustainable, and the top marginal tax rates increased to a range of 46 to 49 percent.

Neither of these partial increases in tax rates was put back into the public education systems in either country, which would have ensured equal opportunity to quality education. Without a strong education system, individuals will join the economic underground, emotionally disengage through the use of drugs, or join a church. It is not a lack of education that makes people religious; it is the lack of hope and justice in the here and now.

That this problem has not been seriously addressed by the left is not surprising; as the left is led by the educated elite, many of whom are taxed at the top marginal rates. Their preferred strategy is to require that social equality be adjudicated by the legal system and delivered by social welfare programs. The problem is that the religious right is stubbornly refusing to accept their offer.

UNWAVERING COMMITMENT TO TRUTH

> The American Republic will endure until the day Congress discovers that it can bribe the public with the public's money —Alexis de Tocqueville.

Against this backdrop of the expanding education gap, another gap was growing. The primary beneficiaries of civil or human rights laws have been the criminally accused, as their due process rights were expanded to protect against wrongful convictions. While the goal of reducing the wrongfully convicted is a worthy objective, the vast majority of cases involve breaches of existing procedural rules and the lack of adequate legal representation for those who cannot afford it; it was not due to the insufficiency of the due process rights. The problem was overworked public defenders with caseloads over 1,000 who were recommending guilty pleas.[9] This problem did not change with the increased rights, it worsened and meanwhile those with the financial means were able to exclude all but the purest evidence, creating two distinct legal systems; one for the rich and one for the poor.

Failure to recognize the true source of the problem has resulted in an even greater divide between the legal concept of guilt understood by the "educated elite", and the popular concept of guilt, as it relates to what actually happened. This lack of allegiance to objective truth and justice is very corrosive to the social contract. The trend is also problematic from an effectiveness perspective because social science research has found that punishment only works as a deterrent when it is swift and certain. The courts are increasingly neither as a result of increased due process rights and the grossly overworked public defenders.

The OJ Simpson trial and Clinton's impeachment are two examples where the public's confidence in legal and political truth was badly damaged. According to a Gallop poll taken in 1995, 73 percent of Americans believed that OJ Simpson would have been found criminally guilty if he was not wealthy.[10] The result is that new guardians of truth have created new venues for selling truth. Nowhere is this more evident than in the rise of shows like "Judge Judy" and "Judge Alex", who gain loyal viewers by showing no patience or mercy for the party caught lying or trying to make technical qualifications. There is market demand for justice.

Recently the Canadian Supreme Court retrenched on some of its stricter interpretations that were eliminating evidence which did not meet Charter standards. This realization only arose though in 2009 when the Court finally realized that its reputation was suffering. In a 4–3 majority decision, the court reversed a long-standing trend by considering the importance to the public of the legal system's reputation. "Because the exclusion of evidence impacts on trial fairness from society's perspective, insofar as it impairs the truth seeking function of trials."[11] The court originally went astray when it used the Charter to punish sloppy police work. While this is a legitimate objective, the court needs to retain its highest commitment to seeking objective truth—to ensure the social contract remains worth keeping. Police corruption needs to be the responsibility of management, elected officials and investigative journalism, not a function of the courts.

In tandem with the courts, however, the media has also lost its commitment to objectivity. The pursuit of truth was abandoned when the traditional media institutions became addicted to the pursuit of profits after their ratings surged by trailing OJ Simpson driving his Bronco. After OJ's trial wrapped up, the monstrous hybrid of entertainment news was created as OJ's prime time was then filled with the relentless coverage of the Jon Benét Ramsey murder investigation.[12] Once the line between entertainment and news had been crossed, an increasingly polarized America effectively eliminated objectivity as a media objective because more ratings and profits lay in presenting politically consistent messages.

In politics, the "old guards"—well-funded public education with academic freedom and the media seeking to uncover truth, were replaced with late-night comedy shows and "entertainment" news. While traditional journalists are dying a slow death, the paparazzi are now making big money for exposing the backsides of celebrities who have mastered the art of promoting their airbrushed perfection on the endless parade of entertainment news shows. According to a Times Magazine poll, Jon Stewart, a pseudo news anchor, is now the most trusted name in news because he exposes the sloppy journalism of mainstream media and regulators. Americans trust Stewart because he is committed to producing comedy and comedy needs truth to be effective.

The demise of objective truth is also defeating federal regulators, who have faced wave after wave of fraudulent regulatory filings and bankruptcies. Regulators don't have much left in their arsenal considering the onerous regulations introduced in the Sarbanes-Oxley Act of 2002 in response to the Enron, Tyco, and WorldCom scandals. A 2008 *Wall Street Journal* editorial stated, "The new laws and regulations have neither prevented frauds nor instituted fairness. But they have managed to kill the creation of new public companies in the U.S., cripple the venture capital business, and damage entrepreneurship. According to the National Venture Capital Association, in all of 2008 there have been just six companies that have gone public. Compare that with 269 IPOs in 1999, 272 in 1996, and 365 in 1986."[13]

Obama's weak negotiations during the banking bailouts points to the government's limited ability or interest in holding executives accountable. Amending corporate law, or restricting predatory lending, would require Republican support, which will not be forthcoming, because the Libertarians have convinced the religious right, that any trust in government is misplaced. The same problem exists for changing contract law that would hold executives and accountants liable to shareholders for accurate financial disclosure or directors liable for negotiating contracts that pay out millions when a CEO is fired for bankrupting a company.

America will continue to flirt with financial ruin until it re-balances the power between employees and shareholders, against the executive management and boards of directors. Free-market theory is based on the assumption of relatively equal information in the negotiating of price. In 1978 the ratio of executive pay to the average worker was 35; by 2005 that ratio was 262, hitting a high of 300 in 2000. For minimum wage, the ratio in 2005 was 821. How can this be happening, in the "information age"? One rationale for such inflated salaries is executives paid $100,000 in tuition fees for their MBAs, which takes us back full circle to rising tuition fees and Jane Jacob's warning that turning education over the private sector would corrupt it.

All this investment in education, and yet executives still can't tell the difference between creating value and shuffling risk around balance sheets. This strategy is bankrupting America. Benjamin Franklin said, "Rebellion to tyrants is obedience to God." The post-secular version is "Rebellion to tyrants is obedience to truth": truth in the numbers, truth in value and truth in the form of real accountability to shareholders and employees. Without an orientation to truth, as Harvey Cox pointed out, there is the risk of "ethical anarchism and metaphysical nihilism":

> Nihilism represents the adolescent phase of the relativization of values. It swings back and forth from a giddy celebration of the freedom man has when the gods are dead to a wistful longing after the return to a world of secure and dependable meanings and norms. In psychoanalytical terms, the nihilist displays a deep ambivalence toward the authority figure represented by God and traditional values. Having rejected the father, he still cannot achieve maturity and self-actualization. Nihilism is therefore some kind

of diabolism. The nihilist uses his newfound freedom from the tyranny of God not to become a true man but to revel in all the things the dead god once forbade.[14]

The religious right is correct in that America cannot afford healthcare or even quality education until America addresses capitalism's monstrous hybrids and raises its top marginal tax rate. The French revolution is a lesson in the consequences of a state losing its ability to tax the rich. The difference between the left and the right lies in where they each see the root of the problem. The left cynically believes that all Republicans are greedy, uneducated or irrational religious zealots. The religious right believes that America has lost respect for God and religion.

The religious right intuitively, even if not rationally, understands the importance of committing to objective truth. Once the traditional liberals in the Democratic Party see the political potential of an alliance with such fiercely loyal and disciplined believers over the issue of secularization, America will be much better equipped to rectify its problem of economic inequality with capitalist, not communist, tools.

Traditional liberals need to understand what the neoconservatives and libertarians discovered and have exploited for the past forty years; that the religious right will sacrifice their economic well-being for their religious beliefs and commitment to one absolute truth. The religious right's desire to be "United under One God", makes more than political sense, it makes economic sense.

The religious right will likely jump to offer their cooperation on healthcare and taxation issues, once they are convinced that the constitutional gains they secured by the currently conservative Supreme Court bench, in the form of secularization, can be protected against secularism. The Cold War cannot officially end until America commits to secularization. If this does not happen, then like the Berlin wall, the American wall fall, because corporate nihilism will bankrupt America with their monstrous hybrids.

UNITED UNDER ONE TRUTH

"United under one God" is not the ignorant rambling of a fear monger—it is a genuine plea to return to the constitutional values of traditional liberalism, but with a modern twist of giving up skepticism. America can no longer afford the luxury of skepticism; it needs all hands on deck to stay afloat during this financial storm.

Political parties will fracture along the lines of secularism versus secularization. Once the tyranny of corporate America has been removed, America will once again excel economically because only in a climate of secularization are individuals truly empowered to take initiative, be creative, compassionate, and open-minded. Secularization was the foundation for that magical combination of hope, individual empowerment, and determination that fueled America's first political and economic era, and so too will it fuel its second. America's adherence to the ideal of separating church and state allowed reason to grow out from the shadow of its much older sibling—religion. America's next wave of secularization will be complete when reason and revelation are genuinely reconciled by American citizens, at which time there will be no need for the wall of separation.

Religious practices will still exist, but the legal and religious moral codes will be consistent. This will happen with a greater understanding of the nature and importance of mythical language. In a consciously secularizing society, citizens are taught how to discuss moral differences by discussing *how* they know things to be true; personal experience, reason or revelation. Progress will come with a fuller understanding the relative strengths and limitations of each form of knowledge, and the necessity of reconciling all three.

Robert Nisbet wrote in 1969 that "achieving the impossible is what the metaphor is all about"[15] and that metaphor is indispensable to both philosophy and religion because it maintains faith in difficult times "as a synthesis of past, present and future."[16] The metaphoric wall's greatest triumph was in crushing the universal belief in the necessity of aligning religious and political powers for civil order. But this accomplishment is now holding America back from realizing its full potential and needs to be replaced by *Secular Hope's* U shaped vision of progress.

NOTES

1. Ian Urbina and Katherine Q. Seelyen, "Senator Goes Face to Face With Dissent" New York Times, August 11, 2009. http://www.nytimes.com/2009/08/12/health/policy/12townhall.html?bl&ex=1250308800&en=7d2839404222733a&ei=5087%0A

2. CNN Political Producer Peter Hamby August 26, 2009 McCain: Health care reform has sparked a 'peaceful revolt' Posted: August 26th, 2009 05:07 AM ET http://politicalticker.blogs.cnn.com/2009/08/26/mccain-health-care-reform-has-sparked-a-peaceful-revolt-2/

3. Eric Heubeck, "The Integration of Theory and Practice: A Program for the New Traditionalist Movement," 2001 by the Free Congress Foundation. Written with Free Congress Foundation founder Paul Weyrich.

4. Max Borders on Tue, 02/24/2009, The Next Right, a grassroots movement to recreate the Republican Party, http://www.thenextright.com/about

5. National Association of Independent Colleges and Universities, President David L. Warren in a News Release dated June 29, 2009, "Private College Tuition Rises at Lowest Rate in 37 Years" http://www.naicu.edu/news_room/private-college-tuition-rises-at-lowest-rate-in-37-years

6. http://www.newsday.com/long-island/nassau/weak-economy-spurs-surge-in-community-college-enrollment-1.1327187

7. According to a Statistics Canada Daily Report of Tuesday, September 27, 2005 http://www.statcan.gc.ca/daily-quotidien/050927/dq050927a-eng.htm

8. Internal Revenue Service Personal Exemptions and Individual Income Tax Rates 1913-2002 http://irs.gov/pub/irs-soi/02inpetr.pdf

9. According to the Testimony before New York State Bar on Wrongful Convictions by Jonathan Gradess, Executive Director of the New York State Defenders Association, February 24, 2009 and the Kaye Commission Report on Indigent Defense, 7. http://www.nysda.org/09_JEGNYSBATaskForceWrongfulConvictions2-24-09.pdf.

10. http//law.umkc.edu/faculty/projects/FTRIALS/Simpson/simpso.htm

11. R. v. Bjelland, 2009 Supreme Court of Canada 38.

12. Thanks to Hany Maurice for this insightful observation.

13. Wall Street Journal December 21, 2008.

14. Harvey Cox, The Secular City (NY: Macmillan Company, 1965) 34.

15. Robert Nisbet, Social Change and History (NY: Oxford University Press, 1969) 241-2.

16. Ibid, 251.

Appendix I – Comparing Assumptions

	Absolute Monotheism	Rational Secularism	Romantic Secularism	Postmodern Secularism	Secularization
Nature of Truth	One Universal Truth	One Universal Truth	Wall splits private/ public truths	Multiple Truths	One Universal Truth
Legitimate Knowledge Sources	Religion Only	Reason Only	Reason, Religion and Personal Experiences	Reason, Experiences and non-monotheistic religions	Reason, Religion and Personal Experiences
Moral Experts	Religious Clergy	Select Academics & Political Leaders	Electorate Judiciary Elected Officials	Judiciary	Electorate
Source of Authority	Divine Right to Rule Scriptures	Specific Theory of Human Nature	Social Contract	Human Rights	Social Contract
Highest Political Virtue	Faith/Belief Obedience	Evidence of Success Right=Might Might=Right	Freedom	Tolerance Diversity Equality	Seeking Universal Truth through Subjective freedom
Problems	No Human Rights	Requires Revolution - no Human Rights	Private/ Public line is crumbling	Excludes Monotheism	Slow Must overcome Skepticism
Examples	Henry VIII, England Taliban, Afghanistan	Soviet & Chinese Communism NaziFascism New Atheists	United States	Canada	United States?

Appendix II –
Monotheism's
Historical Plot of
Hope

Simple Unity – Divine Rulers and Monotheism

In the very beginning "There was no gulf between humans and gods.... The gods and human beings shared the same predicament, the only difference being that the gods were more powerful and immortal"[1] In the very end, there will be no gulf between humans and their natures. In the beginning humans looked to the stars trying to understand and predict the behavior of the gods. In the end, humans will look inside to understand how the world works. In the beginning there was very little notion of the individual because individual survival was so closely tied to the fate of the tribe; in the end, every individual will need to be understood in order to save the human race from extinction.

As man's ability to control nature evolved, psychic dependency on the gods diminished and individuals began to assert themselves. But the transference of trust was slow. Where

environmental conditions were more favorable, humans started
to transfer reverence (and responsibility) from the gods to their
kings. Comparing the ancient civilizations of Mesopotamia and
Egypt, shows that the Egyptians, with the advantage of better
climate and soil, celebrated their kings with elaborate royal
tombs, while the temples of Ur were still dedicated to the gods.

After the ancient civilizations, most kings only believed that
God played a role in their military victories, thus approving their
right to govern. In mythical language cause and effect are not
distinguished. Circular reasoning was common. Correlation was
enough; so might made right and right made might. The common
understanding was that kings were entitled to rule because God
had allowed it to be so.

As Cox pointed out in *The Secular City*, when God spoke
directly to Moses through a burning bush in the desert, a
significant political development occurred. Disregarding the
Egyptian king's monopoly over access to God's will was critical
in sowing the seed of individualism. The significance of the
parable for our purpose is that it represents God bypassing the
established hierarchy of the king and speaking directly to Moses,
a man of little power and social status, giving him the confidence
that he could play a role in God's plans and history. There are a
number of historical figures, such as Martin Luther, and Martin
Luther King Jr. who also listened to their own conscience when
God spoke to them and gathered the confidence to heroically
challenge corrupt authorities.

Many centuries after the time of Moses, the concept of
having two separate moral authorities first emerged when
Christ, as a minority within the minority religion of Judaism,
wisely responded to Pontius Pilate's inquiries into Christ's self-
proclaimed kingship: "My Kingdom is not of this world". Four
hundred years later, when Christianity had grown to become the
official Roman religion in AD 380, it became so much of this
world that Augustine confidently declared that the Church was

not merely standing out of the way of secular rulers but actually had the divine responsibility to oversee them.

But the Christian church could not rest on its temporal alliance with Constantine for long because the downside risk of the divine right to rule becomes evident when empires fall. Consistency requires one to assume that either God is punishing the conquered or they were praying to the wrong God. Just when subjects need religion the most, the myth of divine right to rule creates a religious crisis. When Rome surprisingly fell in 410, the Christian church had to be the cause. In defense of the Church, Augustine wrote *The City of God*, wherein he encouraged Christians to remain faithful by telling them God had not abandoned them, but would deliver his rewards in the afterlife. Augustine saved the Church by arguing that the downfall of Rome was inevitable because it was a human creation, subject to the human life cycle of birth, growth, maturity, and decline. This was the ∩ plot of tragedy and mortality. God and religion were supernatural and therefore could transcend this earthly cycle turning it upside down into a U-shape plot of hope.

DESCENDING THE U – CHALLENGING THE DIVINE RIGHT TO RULE

In today's democracies, the divine right to rule seems naïve for people rationally capable of building such wonders as Westminster Abbey. But given the architectural accomplishments left by most ancient and medieval kings that continue to amaze tourists today, we must admit that these kings did achieve a type of immortality that has eluded most modern political rulers. The ancient cities of Sumer and Ur, the Egyptian and Inca pyramids, and Gothic cathedrals are all marvels of human ingenuity, none of which is remotely possible today as we struggle to repair our roads and bridges in our cookie-cutter suburbs. Myths have a magical way of being ridiculously false and yet amazingly true.

The myth of divine appointment endured for thousands of years because church and state authorities usually balanced each other when corruption got out of control on either side. The king could have you killed only once, but the clergy could doom you to the pits of Hell forever. As long as the subjects of William the Conqueror believed in the power of the Pope, there was an earthly counterbalance to his ruthless ambitions. Kings knew the clergy could undermine their secular power because while royal dynasties came and went, the Church had endured, just as Augustine suggested. The balance was evidenced when, in 1080, the Pope told William he should pull back on his mistreatment of the English. Respectfully treading the line, William cunningly established his own Norman court in England, which would eventually split the ecclesiastical courts away from the state altogether.

The balance of power was often tipped when either a king or a Pope began to think they were more God-like than they actually were, and it was usually the noblemen who benefitted from the skirmishes. Abusive monarchs began to be held accountable to written contracts that limited their power, eventually evolving into constitutional law. One such incident, like so many political changes, was due to sibling rivalry. In 1100, William the Conqueror's estate was distributed to his three sons. Robert, the oldest, inherited Normandy; William II (Rufus) inherited England; and Henry, the youngest, received five thousand pounds and an education. When the middle son Rufus died in a hunting accident while Robert the eldest was away on a crusade, discontented young Henry seized the opportunity to make himself king of England by seeking the support of the local barons and clergy. Rufus had been making a habit of seizing church and private assets, so the barons and Church were willing to crown Henry king only three days after Rufus died in exchange for the *Charter of Liberties*, which limited the absolute power of the king. This statute eventually was revised into the *Magna Carta* in 1215.

Another instance occurred in 1164, when Henry II of was trying legally limiting the political role of the Roman Catholic Church. When success was just one signature away, Henry was confronted by the defiant Thomas Becket, a close, personal friend who Henry had just appointed as Archbishop of Canterbury. Becket's defiance was particularly difficult for Henry to accept because he was a mere commoner. Henry retaliated by charging Becket with treason and misuse of funds. Upon conviction, Becket fled the country and excommunicated supporters of the king. Becket eventually persuaded a reluctant Pope to threaten to excommunicate Henry himself, and the rest of Britain with him, if Henry did not forgive Becket and allow him back into the country. That Henry conceded, speaks to how deeply he believed in the fatal political, if not spiritual, consequences of the Pope condemning he and his subjects to Hell. Individuality was not then fully developed because it was commonly understood that a king was responsible for his subjects' spiritual well-being.[2]

Becket continued to act as Henry's equal until Henry's exasperation inspired a few of Henry's loyal courtiers to take the initiative and murder Becket on Henry's behalf. It was a tragedy for everyone because the murder haunted Henry's conscience and those of his subjects. To make amends, in 1174 Henry took a barefoot pilgrimage to Canterbury, wearing a hair shirt in Becket's memory. After that, the balance of power leaned in the Church's favor for several hundred more years, leading to religious corruption so extreme that Luther (1483-1546), another mere commoner, outdid Becket by daring to suffer the wrath of both Emperor and Pope.

Before Luther's story it must be mentioned that Thomas of Aquinas (1225–1274) was the first Christian writer to explicitly undermine the 'divine appointment' myth. He did so by stating that tyrants, whether they were kings, oligarchs, or democrats, had no legitimate governing authority. Aquinas rationally argued that rulers should be those best capable of identifying and implementing the common good. Aquinas did not intend to usurp from either the Catholic Church or from monarchs their authority, established since days of Constantine. Aquinas merely wanted to place their authority on firmer ground, replacing the myth of divine right to rule, with a rational argument.

Aquinas was comfortable offering a rational basis for the legitimacy of the Church's power because it appeared obvious that the Church met the criteria of being expert in identifying the right path to happiness. He also confirmed that monarchies were superior to democracies because they provided for more stable government and therefore offered better political security to individual subjects. Many of Aquinas' ideas were initially rejected by the Church, and his teachings were not officially adopted by the Catholic Church for another six hundred years—until 1879. Aquinas' ideas did not have a significant impact on other thinkers until the Enlightenment, or on commonly held beliefs until the twentieth century. The tenacious myth of divine appointment continued unchallenged into the sixteenth century.

At the turn of the sixteenth century, Luther, an Augustinian monk, challenged the Pope's monopoly on religious truth at the Diet of Worms by recommending, among other things, that ordinary lay people could rely on their own reading of the Bible. Like many steps toward secularization, Luther wanted to save God but eliminate the corrupt clergy. So Luther argued that corruption had to be prevented by replacing the Pope's interpretation of the scriptures with individual personal access to scripture. Luther's movement gave permission, to those who wanted it, to bypass the priests and have a personal relationship with God. Luther was extremely brave because he could not challenge the Church without also challenging the king's right to rule.

Luther, using Augustine's *The City of God* as the philosophical basis of his argument, significantly furthered the concept of separating church and state. By emphasizing Augustine's separate cities, and the voluntary nature of citizenship in either city, a political solution becomes necessary for those who choose to live in sin, and their punishment can only be the responsibility of the secular state. Essentially, Luther told the church and the state to get out of the business of mandating spiritual morality:

> God has ordained the two governments: the spiritual, which by the Holy Spirit under Christ makes Christians and pious people; and the secular, which restrains the unchristian and wicked so that they are obliged to keep the peace outwardly ... The laws of worldly government extend no farther than to life and property and what is external upon earth. For over the soul God can and will let no one rule but himself. Therefore, where temporal power presumes to prescribe laws for the soul, it encroaches upon God's government and only misleads and destroys souls. We desire to make this so clear that every one shall grasp it, and that the princes and bishops may see what fools they are when they seek to coerce the people with their laws and commandments into believing one thing or another.

Luther's influence spread, and soon there was a demand for Bibles to be written in the English language. When Henry VIII learned that a man named Tyndale was completing an unauthorized translation of the Bible, in 1530 Henry passed a law forbidding translations into the "vulgar language" of English. Luther was excommunicated that same year by Pope Leo X. However, nine years later, Pope Leo refused to grant Henry an annulment from his wife, Catherine of Aragon, not for purely religious reasons but more likely because Catherine's nephew, Charles V, was invading Italy. The annulment would have allowed Henry to produce a legitimate male heir with his mistress, Anne Boleyn. So Luther had a new ally against the Pope and Henry VIII had a biblical argument for overruling the Pope's rejection of his annulment request.

Henry VIII was not entirely disingenuous in his new friendship with Luther—he did reverse his position by trying to free Tyndale from Charles V's impending order of execution. However, after introducing a series of laws that first reduced the powers of the Catholic Church, Henry eventually created the Church of England. Not surprisingly, once Henry was granted his annulment from his own personally appointed Archbishop of Canterbury, he ended his support of the reformation movement. Henry placed himself as the supreme head of the new Anglican Church, and when not all of his subjects enthusiastically embraced him as their new spiritual leader, he passed the *Royal Supremacy Act*, which stated that anyone doubting the monarchy's authority over the Church would be charged with treason, punishable by death. So much for Luther's ideal of a voluntary, personal relationship with God.

Furthermore, when Henry declared that being Catholic was an act of treason, he did not mean substantively; he meant politically. Therefore, most of the Catholic traditions continued in the Anglican Church, much to the annoyance of the Protestant reformers. More importantly, an unanticipated consequence of empowering the reformist movement was that it gave commoners the idea that they could start using the Bible as legitimate justification for demanding that the king and his noblemen uphold Christ's teachings of treating the poor with dignity and respect. Individualism would have to take two steps backwards, before it would regain its momentum and come back twice as strong.

The consequence of empowering the reformist movement in name only threw England into the religious war and turmoil slightly ahead of her European neighbors. Henry's mixed-up religious convictions were his legacy, humanly personified through his three legitimate children, each of whom sat on the throne, thrusting the country back and forth from Protestant, to Catholic, and then back to Protestant, in the space of eleven short years. Political insecurity resulted in Elizabeth I keeping her Catholic first cousin, Mary Queen of Scots, captive for many years, then ordering her murder, cloaking intolerance, bigotry and cruelty in the guise of religious superiority. Mary's murder aside, Elizabeth successfully managed a fine line that kept the peace between the conservative Catholics and the radical Puritans during her 45-year reign, but it was still a criminal act not to attend the Anglican Church. The result being that many Scottish and Irish subjects fled to America instead of changing their religious beliefs.

Against the Western backdrop of increasing democratization, a new source of political legitimacy was required to replace the myth of the divine right of kings. The Jewish covenant with God was first secularized by Aquinas, and then by Hobbes, Locke, and Rousseau as variations of the social contract theory. The covenant was secularized by replacing a promise to be loyal to God with an agreement to be loyal to the sovereign as long as the sovereign secured physical and spiritual well-being. This transition occurred most prominently in America where the people formed a government of the people, for the people.

Western descent from our mythical understanding of the divine right of kings to Benjamin Franklin's motto "Rebellion to tyrants is obedience to God" happened because the synergistic relationship between church and state resulted in corruption more than peace. The journey can be summarized as an uneasy balance of power that failed to prevent abuses by both kings and clerics such that eventually Henry VIII dared to endure excommunication and create his own church. Henry was confident enough to take the risk, not because he stopped believing in God, but because he had a quotation from the Bible that said he never should have been allowed to marry his dead brother's wife in the first place. While Henry VIII thought he solved his succession issues by producing a legitimate male heir, he inadvertently sowed the seeds of the British monarchy's decline, because he taught his subjects that challenging authority was not always disastrous, especially if you could get access to original documents that proved the official position was not as historically sacred as the holders of power would lead you to believe.

Henry's now unfettered power resulted in a flurry of executions, and in desperation, many of the convicted pulled out the dusty *Magna Carta,* in order to find something that could hold Henry accountable. They were unsuccessful, but the statute was brought back into the public memory and developed an exaggerated, but enduring, reputation for empowering subjects to overthrow a king that disobeyed the laws of the land. Once the mythical connection between God and king was undermined, by Henry placing himself as the head of the Anglican Church, the replacement of the British monarchy with an elected Parliament was not far off. Feudal landlords continued to gain rights that eventually became the rights of Parliament, and the Supremacy of Parliament.

One hundred years later, in 1648, the Peace of Westphalia marked the official end of the Catholic Church's political power because both Catholic and Protestant princes agreed to disregard the protests of the Pope in signing the treaties of Munster and Osnabruck.[3] Monarchs now needed a new source of legitimacy, and in the midst of a civil war, Thomas Hobbes resurrected the Judaic notion of a special covenant with God to replace the myth of the divine right of kings. Ironically, however, while Hobbes graciously endowed all the king's subjects with a natural, God-given freedom that allowed them to choose the government best able to secure their interests, Hobbes then insisted that it had to be an irrevocable contract with an absolute ruler and with no balance of power.

Hobbes, like Aquinas, merely changed the justification for tyrannical rule. But Hobbes' theory required complete and absolute control by the sovereign, even over matters of the Church, because human nature was naturally violent. This idea was much more commonly accepted in the sixteenth century than it is today. But Hobbes knew that his political theory would be problematic for Christians with a higher moral allegiance to God over a king. He never successfully resolved the conflict, which proved to be the downfall of his constitutional teachings.

The important point is that absolute tyrants no longer needed to rely upon the myth of divine appointment to justify their existence; they had rational reasons, supported by the Christian doctrine of original sin. Hobbes' fate is of interest today because he would have predicted that the separation of church and state would not have worked in America because American Christians, unlike English Christians, have a higher allegiance to God when state and religion conflict as they do over the issue of same-sex marriage. Political power in America is grounded in the rule of law as expressed by the Constitution; monarchies are grounded in myth of the divine right to rule.

CONSTITUTIONAL SUPREMACY

It was not the Enlightenment thinkers like Locke (1632–1704) and Voltaire (1694–1778) who eventually overturned Hobbes' justifications for absolute monarchical rule; it was romanticism. Jean-Jacques Rousseau (1712–1778) had to first convince religious believers that human nature is good and that it is institutions that corrupt men by oppressing them. The French and Americans were now armed with rational principles grounded in Christianity and were ready to free their people from aristocratic tyranny. Constitutional law decentralized monarchies into oligarchies, which eventually resulted in universal suffrage. Individualism was just beginning to crest when America decided to revolt against King George III and eventually Americans had the rare opportunity to create their Constitution afresh.

In 1779 Thomas Jefferson and John Adams developed two different constitutional models for protecting religious liberty for their respective states of Virginia and Massachusetts. A comparison of their different approaches is instructive to the debate today. Both men believed that religion had a critical role to play in society, but that it was necessary to limit the role of religion in state affairs. It helps to understand their respective religious views in order to appreciate the reasons for their different proposals. While Jefferson is often revered by atheists, Jefferson was a Deist. Deists believe that God created the earth (monotruists) but then abandoned it:

> Almighty God has created the free mind" Jefferson wrote. "[A]ll attempts to influence it by temporal punishments, or burthens, or by civil incapacitations, tend only to beget habits of hypocrisy and meanness, and are a departure from the plan of the holy author our religion....[4]

Jefferson, echoing John Locke, thus argued that freedom of conscience was a natural right given by God to each citizen and the state should not interfere with beliefs at all, in any way. Jefferson's views, heartily supported and furthered by the Baptist community, eventually became simplified into the metaphor of "a wall of separation" between church and state, after Jefferson used the phrase in a letter to the Danbury Baptists in 1802. While the Deists and the Danbury Baptists had very different objectives, they formed a political coalition because they shared an interest in the full separation of church and state. The Deists wanted to free the development of reason from religious control, while the devoted religious Protestants wanted to ensure that their religions remained free from political corruption, and wanted to ensure that more popular traditional religions were not supported with state funds or given any other advantages.

In contrast, John Adams was of Puritan descent. That said Adams still believed that blasphemy laws were an embarrassment because Adams believed that reason and Christianity could be reconciled – so he was not against the objectives of free-thinking Deists. He was concerned, however, with a purely rational defense of the Republican values of freedom and equality:

159

The notion that a state and society could remain neutral and purged of any religion was, for Adams, a philosophical fiction. Absent a commonly adopted set of values and beliefs, politicians would inevitably hold out their own private convictions as public ones. It was thus essential for each community to define the basics of its public religion. In Adam's view, the creed of this public religion was honesty, diligence, devotion, obedience, virtue and love of God, neighbor and self.[5]

In a letter to Jefferson, Adams predicted the modern debate:

Every Species of these Christians would persecute Deists, as [much] as either Sect would persecute another, if it had unchecked and unbalanced Power. Nay, the Deists would persecute Christians, and Atheists would persecute Deists, with as unrelenting Cruelty, as any Christians would prosecute them or one another. *Know Thyself, Human Nature!*[6] [Emphasis added].

Adams' argument for a mild establishment of religion also stemmed from the belief that "there was no stronger cement of society" than religious oaths.[7] Adams believed that citizens needed to believe in something higher than themselves, so amongst other requirements, Adams' draft constitution had a clause requiring state officials to swear a religious oath to the Christian religion and profess persuasion of its truth. John Witte Jr. summarized Adams' approach very well:

Too little religious freedom, Adams insisted, is a recipe for hypocrisy and impiety. But too little religious freedom is an invitation to depravity and license. Too firm a religious establishment breeds coercion and corruption. But too little religious establishment allows secular prejudices to become constitutional prerogatives. Somewhere between these extremes, Adams believed, a society must find its balance.[8]

Not surprisingly, at the national level Adams' "a most mild and equitable establishment of religion" gave way to the coalition's simpler wall of separation. It is ironic that by adopting Jefferson's separation of church and state the common denominator of religious doctrines was found. By slowly culling religious beliefs from the common law, the religious community finally found a common issue which they could not accept: the issue of same-sex marriage. Neither abortion nor capital punishment had this unifying power. In another ironic twist, however, the cost of Jefferson's approach is that Americans lost their common belief in the critical role of religion in determining moral behavior. Unlike 1791, the debate today is no longer between different Christian denominations but is between the two beneficiaries of Jefferson's wall of separation, the Baptists and scientists.

CROSSING THE U - FRAGMENTATION, CONFLICT & DESPAIR

In addition to decentralizing political power, Western culture also continued to splinter religiously; Christianity from Judaism, Islam from Christianity and Judaism, modern Judaism from Orthodox, Anglican from Catholicism, and so on—ultimately into the thousands of religious denominations and sects that exist today, each spawning many religious conflicts and wars along the way. There is no doubt that on the mythical plot of monotheism: we are somewhere on the bottom of the U, in a state of fragmentation, diversification, individualism and conflict.

The question is: Where do we go from here? Some want to regress to monotheism. Most academics believe that moral relativism is as good as it gets and therefore insist upon educational programs teaching tolerance. The potential for a politically unifying truth is not seriously contemplated by either side, largely because the metaphoric wall has convinced most of us that it is not possible to integrate the diversity of religious and secular beliefs, partly because modernity has been so consistently paired with secularism, but also, sadly, because trust has been so badly eroded between the two sides.

ASCENDING THE U – DARING TO CROSS THE THRESHOLD OF HOPE[9]

To restate the mythos in the language of the New Testament:

> Jesus then said to the Jews who had believed in him "If you continue in my word, then you are truly my disciples, and you will know the truth, and the truth will make you free."[10]

Secularization seeks one truth through understanding and respecting human diversity. It neither rejects nor imposes religious beliefs. It transcends religion through rational understanding. If there is agreement that one truth underlying human morality exists, a society can start to climb back up the second arm of the U to a much more complex understanding of not only other religions, but to a further understanding of how reason, revelation, and personal experiences can interact to determine a universal understanding of human nature. Secularization restricts the political power of religion in order to give reason sufficient independence to cull the political contamination out of religion, as well as allowing it to mature to the point of being able to rationally articulate the wisdom of myths that persist in a secular world.

Secularism, with the goal of extinguishing religion, actually extinguishes hope and stops the secularization process at the bottom of the U. Secularism, not wanting to go backward or forward, sacrifices both simple and complex truth. Diversity and tolerance become the highest social goals possible. By aligning secularism with modernity, we have limited our potential to mere tolerance. Secularism trades hope for tolerance. As Thomas Aquinas said, "To sin is to lose one's potential".

Many believers are reverting to fundamental or evangelical monotheistic religions because they don't know any other way to reject secularism. They are not rejecting reason per se, but they intuitively understand that current political reasoning squashes hope in the possibility of reconciliation. Fundamentalists are reacting to secularism by insisting on the literal translation of their scriptures because they would rather be hopeful, rather than rational. This is why they try so hard to rationalize religion's story of creation as an alternative to evolution.

Secularization is a long-term collective commitment to the process of reconciling reason, faith, and collective personal experiences. It is tolerance in the face of uncertainty, existing for the purpose of achieving certainty, not for the sake of moral relativism, liberty, or equality. Western secularization encourages the continued freedom of conscience in its fullest sense— freedom of individual experiences, reason, and faith, such that every individual might reconcile their head with their heart and their body. Individuals are then granted the responsibility of contributing to our collective understanding of human nature through political and legal participation. In 1790, Supreme Court Justice James Wilson articulated the search for the will of God (or truth) this way:

> How shall we, in particular cases, discover the will of God? We discover it by our conscience, our reason, and by the Holy Scriptures. The law of nature and the law of revelation are both divine; they flow, through different channels, from the same adorable source. It is indeed, preposterous

to separate them from each other. The object of both is—to discover the will of God—and both are necessary for the accomplishment of that end.[11]

NOTES

1. Armstrong, Karen, A History of God, (New York: Alfred A. Knopf, 1993) 9.

2. Stimson, Elam Rush, History of the Separation of Church and State in Canada (Toronto, 1887) 15.

3. Hastings, James History of Christianity, 1650–1950— Secularization of the West (New York: Ronald Press, 1956) 6.

4. John Witte Jr. "A most Mild and Equitable Establishment of Religion" John Adams and the Massachusetts Experiment", in Religion in the New Republic, ed. James H. Hutson, (ed.), p.3 (Lanthan MD: Rowman and Littlefield Publishers, Inc., 2000).

5. John Witte Jr., "A Most Mild..." 3.

6. Ibid, 3-4.

7. Ibid, 7.

8. Ibid, 30-1.

9. This title is respectfully acknowledges and recommends the book, Crossing the Threshold of Hope, which is a long interview with Pope John Paul II prepared by Vittorio Messori (Knopf: 1994).

10. Holy Bible (Revised Standard Version, 1971) John Chapter 8:31–2.

11. James Wilson, "The Laws of Nature," 1790 Hutson, Our Sacred Honor, 171.

GLOSSARY

Monotheism
: A religious belief that there is one universal truth underpinning morality, that religion is the only legitimate means of understanding and seeking that truth, and that only one religion has identified the correct path to universal truth.

Monotruism
: The belief that there is one universal truth regarding human nature that underpins morality.

Postmodern Secularism
: A constitutional model that holds tolerance and diversity as the highest political values and therefore religious freedoms should not be protected if it asserts a moral absolute. This model is based on the assumption that there is no objective moral truth, only irreconcilable multiple truths.

Rational Secularism	A constitutional model based on the assumption that religion and reason are irreconcilable and therefore religion must be culturally extinguished.
Romantic Secularism	A constitutional model that holds that the highest moral values are individual freedom and equality, and that the state needs to be neutral with regard to spiritual beliefs such that individuals are free to pursue, and vote according to, their own versions of universal moral truth.
Secular	A political system that is independent from religious control and may or may not protect religious freedoms.
Secularization	A political commitment to develop a universal moral code based on a rational understanding of human nature by allowing for a rational reconciliation of religious teachings with the full diversity of human experiences.

Tolerance	An individual suspending judgment toward other's beliefs or nonharmful behavior because there is no belief in an objective truth OR because one recognizes that there are significant aspects of human nature that are not yet rationally understood and therefore they cannot conclusively justify moral judgment.
Toleration	A state suspending judgment toward a citizen's beliefs that may be causing the individual or others spiritual harm but not any physical or economic harm.

BIBLIOGRAPHY

Adams, J.F., ed. *The Works of John Adams*. Vol. 4. Boston: Little and Brown, 1856.

Ahmed, Hasanuddin. *Introducing the Qur'an*. New Delhi: Goodword Books, 2004.

Ali, Asghar. *Islam and Secularism*. http://geocities.com//indiafas/India/islam_&_secularism.htm (accessed August 2009).

Aquinas, Thomas. *Aquinas, Selected Philosophical Writings*. Translated by Timothy McDermott. New York : Oxford University Press, 1993.

Armstrong, Karen. *A History of God, The 4,000 - Year Quest of Judaism, Christianity and Islam*. New York: Ballantine Books, 1993.

—. *The Battle for God, A History of Fundamentalism*. New York: Ballantine Books, 2000.

Asad, Talal, interview by Saba Mahmood. *Modern power and the reconfiguration of religious traditions* http://www.standford.edu/group/SHR/5-1/text/toc.html, (February 27, 1996).

Benson, Iain. "The Freedom of Conscience and Religion." *Emory International Law Review* 21 (Spring 2007).

Berger, Peter, ed. *The Desecularization of the World: Resurgent Religion and World Politics.* Grand Rapids: William B. Eerdmans, 1999.

—. "Secularism in Retreat." *The National Interest,* Winter 1996: 47.

Bloom, Allan. *The Closing of the American Mind - How Higher Education has failed Democracy and Impoverished the Souls of Today's Students.* New York: Simon & Shuster, 1987.

—. *Love and Friendship* New York: Simon & Schuster, 1993.

Blumenthal, Sidney. *The Rise of the Counter Establishment, The Conservative Ascent to Political Power.* New York: Union Square Press, 1986.

Bly, Robert. *The Sibling Society.* Reading, MA: Addison-Wesley Publishing Company, 1996).

Borders, Max. "The Next Right, A Grassroots movement to Recreate the Republican Party." http://www/thenextright.com/about, February 24, 2009.

Bouchard, Gerard, and Charles Taylor. *Building the Future, A Time for Reconciliation Report.* http://accommodements.qc.ca/documentation/rapports/rapport-final-integral-en.pdf.

Brown, Wendy. *Regulating Aversion, Tolerance in the Age of Identity and Empire.* Princeton: Princeton University, 2006.

Brownstein, Ronald. *The Second Civil War, How Extreme Partisanship has Paralyzed Washington and Polarized America.* New York: Penguin Books, 2007.

Cahill, Thomas. *The Gift of the Jews How a Tribe of Desert Nomads Changed the Way Everyone Thinks and Feels*. New York: Doubleday, 1998.

Campbell, Joseph. *Myths to Live By*. New York: Penguin Compass, 1972.

Casanova, Jose. *Public Religions in the Modern World*. Chicago: University of Chicago Press, 1994.

Chamberlain v. Surrey School District 36. 28654 (Supreme Court of Canada, December 20, 2002).

Cox, Harvey. *Religion in the Secular City, Toward a Postmodern Theology*. New York: Simon & Shuster, 1984.

—. *The Future of Faith*. New York: HarperCollins, 2009.

—. *The Secular City*. New York: MacMillian Company, 1965.

De Beer, E.S. *The Correspondence of John Locke*. Oxford: Clarendon Press, 1989.

Dunn, Richard, S. *The Age of Religious Wars, 1559-1715*. New York: W.W. Norton, 1979.

Ellis, Joseph J. *Founding Brothers The Revolutionary Generation*. New York: First Vintage Books, 2002.

Esposito, John, and Tamini Azzam (eds.). *Islam and Secularism in the Middle East*. London: Hurst & Co., 2000.

Frankfort, Henri. *The Birth of Civilization in the Near East*. New York: Doubleday Anchor, 1956.

Fraser, A.C., ed. *An Essay Concerning Human Understanding by John Locke*. Vol. 2. Toronto: Dover Publications, 1959.

Friedman, Thomas. "This Fake News Report is Only Too True." *New York Times*, October 25, 2005.

Frye, Northrop. *The Great Code, The Bible and Literature.* Toronto : Penguin, 1990.

—. *The Secular Scripture: A Study of the Structure of Romance.* Cambridge: Harvard University Press, 1976.

—. *Words with Power, Being a Second Study of the Bible and Literature.* New York: Harcourt Brace Jovanovich, Publishers, 1990.

Goodman, L..E.. *The God of Abraham* New York and Oxford: Oxford University Press, 1996.

Gradess, Jonathan. "Testimony Before New York Bar on Wrongful Convictions." Albany: http://www.nysda.org/09_ JEGNYSBATaskForceWrongfulConvictions2-24-09.pdf, 2009.

Habermas, Jurgen. *Religion and Rationality, Essays on Reason, God and Modernity.* Cambridge: Polity Press, 2002.

Halpin, John, and Karl Agne. *State of American Political Ideology 2009: A National Study of Values and Beliefs.* http://www.americanprogress.org/publicsearch/?text=state+of+American+Political+Ideology+2009: Centre for American Progress.

Hamby, Peter. *McCain: Health care reform has sparked a 'peaceful" reovolt'.* August 26th, 2009. http://politicalticker.blogs.cnn.com/2009/08/26/mccain-health-care-reform-has-sparked-a-peaceful-revolt-2/ (accessed August 27, 2009).

Harris, Sam. *The End of Faith, Religion, Terror and the Future of Reason.* New York: W.W. Norton, 2004 .

Harvey, Bob. *The Future of Religion, Interviews with Christians on the Brink.* Ottawa: Novalis, 2001.

Hastings, James. *History of Christianity, 1650-1950-Secularization of the West.* New York: Ronald Press, 1956.

Hatch, Nathan. *The Democratization of American Christianity.* New Haven : Yale University, 1989.

Heubeck, Eric. *The Integration of Theory and Practice: A Program for the New Traditionalist Movement.* Free Congress Foundation, Available at http://www.yuricareport.com/Dominionism/FreeCongressEssay.html, 2001.

Hitchens, Christopher. *god is not Great, How Religion Poisons Everything.* New York : McClelland & Stewart, 2007.

"Holy Bible, Revised Standard Edition." 1971.

Holyoake, G. Jacob. *English Secularism: A Confession of Belief.* Chicago: Open Court Publishing Company, 1896.

—. *Rationalism.* London: J. Watson, 1845.

Huntington, Samual, P. "The Clash of Civilizations?" *Foreign Affairs,* 1993: http://www.foreignaffairs.com/articles/48950/samuel-p-huntington/the-clash-of-civilizations.

Huntington, Samuel P. *The Clash of Civilizations and the Remaking of World Order.* New York: Simon & Shuster, 1996.

Hutson, James H., ed. *Religion in the New Republic, Faith in the Founding of America.* Lanthan, MD: Rowman ad Littlefield, 2000.

Internal Revenue Service. "Personal Exemptions and Individual Income Tax Rates 1913-2002." http://irs.gov/pub/irs-soi/02inpetr.pdf.

International Convenant on Political and Civil Rights. 694/1996 (United Nations, May 11, 1999).

International Progress Organization . *The Concept of Monotheism in Islam and Christianity Papers*. International Symposium, Rome : http://i-o-p.org/islam-christianity-contents. htm, 1981.

Kaufman, Jason. *The Origins of Canadian and American Political Differences*. Cambridge: Harvard University Press, 2009.

Koch, Adrienne, and William Peden, . *The Life and Selected Writings of Thomas Jefferson*. New York: Modern Library, 2004.

Lawyers Gazette. "Equality Rights Face Challenge from Other Rights." Fall/Winter 2005: 11.

Lee, Alvin A., and Jean O'Grady, . *Collected Works of Northrop Frye*. Vol. 4. Toronto: University of Toronto Press, 2000.

Lewis, Bernard. *The Crisis of Islam*. New York: Random House, 2004.

—. "The Revolt of Islam- When did the conflict with the West begin, and how could it end?" *The New Yorker*, November 19, 2001.

Lewis, Bernard, and Buntzie Ellis Churchill. *Islam: The Religion and the People*. New Jersey: Wharton School, 2008.

Locke, John. *An Essay Concerning Human Understanding*. Edited by John W. Yolton. London: Everyman, 1993.

Metro News. "Celebrating marriage across Canada." June 23, 2009.

Murphy, Andrew. *Prodigal Nation*. New York: Oxford, 2009.

Murphy, Andrew R. "Tolerance, Toleration and the Liberal Tradition." *Polity* 9 (1997).

Newport, Frank. *Religious Identity: States Differ Widely.* http://www.gallup.com/poll/122075/Religious-Identity-States-Differ-Widely.aspx?, August 2009.

Niebuhr, Richard. *The Meaning of Revelation.* New York: MacMillian, 1941.

Nisbet, Robert. *Social Change and History, Aspects of Western Theory of Development.* New York: Oxford University Press, 1969.

Norris, Pippa, and Robert Inglehart. "Gods, Guns and Gays, Supply and Demand of religion in the US and Western Europe." 2004. http://ksghome.harvard.edu/~pnorris/Acrobat/APSA%20 2004%20Secularization.pdf (accessed August 2009).

Pettinicchio, David. "Do Canadians Want Same-Sex Marriage Legislation?: The role of Parties, Interest Groups and Public Opinion in the Enactment of the Civil Marriage Act." *Annual Meeting of the American Sociological Association* . Montreal, Quebec: http://www.allacademic.com/meta/p103645.index.html, 2006. 3.

Pew Forum on Religion and Public Life Survey. *U.S. Religious Lanscape Survey, 2009.* http://pewforum.org/docs/?DocID=265, 2009.

Pew Research Centre. *American Mobility, Who Moves, Who Stays Put and Where is Home?* . http://pewsocialtrends.org/assets/pdf/Movers-and-Stayers.pdf, December 2008.

Pew Research Centre Publications. *Gay Marriage and Civil Unions.* http://pewresearch.org/pubs/1375gay-marriage-civil-unions-opinion, 2009.

Plato. *The Republic and other Works.* Translated by B. Jowett. New York : Random House , 1973.

Pope John Paul II. *Fides et Ratio, Encyclical Letter.* Vatican City, 1998.

R. v. Big M Drug Mart. 18125 (Supreme Court of Canada, April 24, 1985).

R. v. Bjelland. 32446 (Supreme Court of Canada, July 30, 2009).

Rabb, Theodore K. *The Struggle for Stability in Early Modern Europe.* New York: Oxford University Press, 1975.

Rawls, John. *Lectures on the History of Moral Philosophy.* Cambridge: Harvard University Press, 2000.

—. *Political Liberalism.* New York: Columbia University Press, 1993.

Salman, Sheik. *Islam and Secularism.* 2008. islamtoday.com (accessed August 2009).

Saul, Ralston. *The Unconscious Civilization.* Toronto : Anansi, 1995.

Seeskin, Kenneth. *Jewish Philosophy in a Secular Age.* Albany: State University of New York Press , 1990.

Smith, Huston. *The World's Religions.* New York: Harper Collins, 1991.

Statistics Canada. *2001 Census Report.* http://www12.statcan. gc.ca/census-recensement/index-eng.cfm.

—. *Daily Report,* September 27, 2005: http://www.statcan. gc.ca/daily-quotidien/050927/dq050927a-eng.htm.

Stimson, Elam Rush. *History of the Separation of Church and State in Canada.* Toronto: http://openlibrary.org/b/

OL7126946M/History_of_the_separation_of_church_and_state_in_Canada, 1887.

Taylor, Charles. *A Secular Age*. Cambridge: Belnap Press, 2007.

—. *The Malaise of Modernity*. Toronto: House of Anansi Press, 1991.

Tribe, Laurence H. *The Invisible Constitution*. New York : Oxford University Press, 2008.

Tuck, Richard, ed. *Hobbes Leviathan, Revised Student Edition*. New York: Cambridge University Press, 1996.

Tucker, Robert C. (ed). *The Marx-Engels Reader*. New York : W.W. Norton, 1978.

Urbina, Ian, and Katherine Q. Seelyen. "Senator Goes Face to Face with Dissent." *New York Times*, August 11, 2009.

Voltaire. *Letter to Frederick II of Prussia*. 1767.

Warren, David L. "Private College Tuition Rises at Lowest Rate in 37 Years." *News Release from National Association of Independent Colleges and Universities*. http://www.naicu.edu/news_room/private-college-tuition-rises-at-lowest-rate-in-37-years, June 29, 2009.

Williams, David, ed. *Voltaire, Political Writings*. New York: Cambridge University Press, 1994.

Wilson, James. "The Laws of Nature." In *The Collected Works of James Wilson*, by Kermit L. Hall and Mark David Hall. Indianapolis: Liberty Fund, 2007.

Wolfe, Alan. "The Coming Religious Peace." *Atlantic Monthly*, March 2008.

—. *The Future of Liberalism.* New York: Alfred A. Knopf, 2009.

INDEX